The Nature of Accounting Regulation

Accounting standards are an essential element in the regulation of current financial reporting. Standard setters promulgate such standards, and companies and professional accountants follow them in preparing financial reports. Although much has been written about the history of standard setting, the conceptual underpinnings of accounting standards, the process of setting them, and whether such standards should be 'rules-based' or 'principles-based,' there has been little written about the kind of thing they are. This book examines the nature of accounting standards and the very idea of a rule, of implementation guidance, and of the objectives that are included in them. It enables the reader to grasp the reasons for promulgating standards, the role of the conceptual framework in setting standards in an institutional context, and the kind of rules that are useful in regulating financial reporting. The insights provided by this examination are used to throw light on the distinction between 'principles-based' and 'rules-based' standards and on the nature of 'good' accounting standards.

Ian Dennis is a senior lecturer in the Accounting, Finance and Economics Department at Oxford Brookes University Business School. He is also an Adjunct Associate Professor at the Norwegian School of Economics.

Routledge Studies in Accounting

The Nature of Accounting Regulation

Ian Dennis

Routledge
Taylor & Francis Group

NEW YORK AND LONDON

First published 2014
by Routledge
711 Third Avenue, New York, NY 10017

Simultaneously published in the UK
by Routledge
2 Park Square, Milton Park, Abingdon, Oxon OX14 4RN

*Routledge is an imprint of the Taylor & Francis Group,
an informa business*

Library of Congress Cataloging-in-Publication Data

Dennis, Ian.
   The nature of accounting regulation / by Ian Dennis. — 1 Edition.
     pages cm. — (Routledge studies in accounting ; 14)
   Includes bibliographical references and index.
1. Accounting.   2. Accounting—Law and legislation.   I. Title.
   HF5636.D46 2013
   657.02'18—dc23
   2013007409

ISBN: 978-0-415-89195-0 (hbk)
ISBN: 978-0-203-79603-0 (ebk)

Typeset in Sabon
by Apex CoVantage, LLC

Printed and bound in the United States of America by Publishers Graphics,
LLC on sustainably sourced paper.

Contents

1   Introduction

This book is about the nature of accounting regulation. 'Regulation' has been defined as 'the imposition of constraints upon the preparation, content and form of external reports by bodies other than the preparers of the reports, or the organizations and the individual for which the reports are prepared' (Taylor and Turley, 1986, p. 61). Given this definition, regulation can be undertaken by various bodies. Legislatures can impose constraints on external reporting through the law. In the UK this is evident in the Companies Acts. Legal regulation of financial reporting is not directly examined in this book. Instead the book focuses on the kind of regulation that is imposed by standard setting bodies and, in the case of the UK and the EU, may be adopted by legislatures. As has been observed, 'the recent history of accounting . . . has been marked by the rapid and continuing promulgation of accounting standards' (West, 2003, p. 1). In the UK the standards promulgated by the International Accounting Standards Board (IASB) as a result of EU decisions and in the U.S. by the Financial Accounting Standards Board (FASB) are central to the regulation of financial reporting for companies listed on stock exchanges. Although the examination of accounting regulation may be relevant to financial reporting in countries other than the UK or EU countries, issues that are particular to them are not analysed. Entities whose financial reports are not regulated by these standard setting bodies are not specifically considered.

WHAT THE BOOK IS *NOT* ABOUT

It might appear rather negative to begin a book by stating what it is *not about*. The problem with accounting regulation is that it is a large topic, and there are a number of important areas of academic research which adopt different methods of enquiry that could be covered by an examination of the nature of accounting regulation. All the approaches to research in this area and the questions asked in these enquiries cannot be considered in a book of this size. It is better to come clean and indicate what will not be considered rather than to disappoint expectations. This will hopefully forestall the kind of objections to the research that amounts to criticism that is, in essence, 'I would like you to have considered . . .' or 'Why haven't you done it like this . . . ?' At least stating what is not covered at the outset will allow readers to decide whether or not to continue reading after the first few pages.

Other things that will not be considered in the book include the question of why we need to regulate financial reporting in the first place. There is a large literature that considers the arguments for and against regulating financial reporting (see the review by Bushman and Landsman, 2010). This literature is not examined in the book. There is regulation of financial reporting, and it happens through the promulgation of accounting standards. The book is not concerned with the question of whether or not there should be such regulation. The book does not get involved in the question of whether or not standard setting is political. It is accepted that financial reporting has 'economic consequences' (Zeff, 1978) and that political considerations may be involved in standard setting (Solomons, 1978; Zeff, 2002; Moran, 2010). Standard setting is an intentional action, and there can be a number of different motivations that give rise to different descriptions of what they are doing. This book takes seriously the suggestion that standard setters set standards by considering 'principles' in a conceptual framework. It therefore takes seriously the idea that an important reason for the actions of standard setting involves such a framework. This is not to discount the fact that there may be other motivations as well. It would only follow that considering the motives provided by a conceptual framework would be pointless if they played no part, or very little part, in explaining or justifying or giving reasons for the action of standard setting. The book does not review the history of standard setting in any detail. This is well covered by accounting historians (Zeff, 1972; Zeff, 1999). It acknowledges that standards set by the IASB and the FASB are important determinants of financial reporting and does not explore how this state of affairs came about.

WHAT THE BOOK IS ABOUT

Having stated what the book is not about, the contribution of the book and the areas that are examined will now be described. Given that financial reporting is regulated, the nature of this activity and the constraints that are imposed by accounting standards are examined. Chapter 2 starts with the obvious point that accounting and financial reporting involve intentional actions. The nature of intentional actions is explained, and the role of practical reasoning in arriving at a desire to perform such actions is examined. The insight that accounting and financial reporting are rule-governed is explored. The practical reasoning to a desire to do something that is in accord with a rule involves taking the rule as part of the reason for performing such actions. Chapter 3 goes on to examine the nature of rules and of practices of following rules. Different practices are identified. It is suggested that financial reporting is an institutional or legal practice where the reasons individuals undertake the actions that constitute financial reporting include the desire to act in accordance with rules established by institutions or the legislature. Where this is the case, examining the reasons for particular actions involves considering not just why individuals follow such rules but also why institutions like standard setters promulgate the rules preparers and accountants want to follow. This leads to a consideration of accounting theories in chapter 4. Two broad approaches to accounting theorizing are examined. One looks at accounting theories as providing general rules from which the more specific rules included in accounting standards are derived. Another approach considers that accounting theories provide reasons for adopting specific rules by identifying what is wanted in promulgating such rules. These reasons constitute premises in practical reasoning to the promulgation of rules by standard setters. Conceptual frameworks in accounting and financial reporting are explained by reference to these two kinds of theorizing. 'Principles' in a conceptual framework can be understood either as general rules that underpin more specific rules or as reasons for adopting specific rules. This provides insight into what is meant by normative theorising in accounting. It also provides one understanding of what it means for the rules in accounting standards to be 'principles-based'. The nature of the reasoning from 'principles' to specific rules is also examined. It is suggested that the model of such reasoning is not deductive but of some other kind. This throws light on the kinds of statements that are included in a conceptual framework and on the role of judgement that must be exercised by the standard setter in reasoning to accounting standards. The kinds of rules that are derived from a conceptual framework are examined in chapter 5. Two different conceptions of rules are identified that deal in different ways with the problem that particular rules may not fulfil the desires that constitute the reasons for their promulgation. A further problem with rules is explored in chapter 6. The language used to express the rules in accounting standards may be vague or indeterminate. The use of explanatory guidance in such standards to overcome these problems is explored. The implications of the analysis in these chapters for the nature of accounting standards are drawn in chapter 7. The anatomy of standards is described. Standards can include objectives, rules and explanatory guidance that deal with the problems of standards setting identified in the previous chapters. The book finishes with drawing out the implications for standard setters of the analysis of the nature of accounting regulation through accounting standards.

THE METHOD IN THE BOOK

The book makes a contribution to understanding the nature of accounting standards and the use of conceptual frameworks in setting accounting standards. The repeated references to questions about 'the nature' of intentional actions, practical reasoning, rules and practices of following rules, theorizing about accounting, 'principles', 'conceptual frameworks', 'principles-based' standards and implementation guidance are meant to indicate that the approach to considering the nature of accounting regulation in this book uses the method of *conceptual enquiry*. Power writes that 'little attention has been given to the role and status of what might be called "conceptual considerations" in financial reporting' (Power, 1993, p. 44). In particular, he argues that there has been a failure to make adequate enquiries into the nature of the concept of a 'conceptual framework' for accounting. Wittgenstein's philosophical method might be called *conceptual enquiry*, and this kind of enquiry is made in this book in relation to the concepts used to explain aspects of accounting regulation. It includes the idea that such regulation proceeds from consideration of the 'principles' in the conceptual framework. Wittgenstein once observed that 'concepts lead us to make investigations; are the expression of our interest, and direct our interest' (Wittgenstein, 1953, §570). The idea that standard setting involves reasoning from 'principles' in a conceptual framework to the intentional action of promulgating rules in accounting standards that include objectives and implementation guidance makes use of a number of concepts, such as 'principles', conceptual frameworks, intentional actions and rules. All these throw light on another concept—that is, the concept of accounting regulation. If standard setters are interested in and directed in their regulation of accounting by such concepts then it is important that they are clearly understood. As will be argued in the book, this is seldom the case. Conceptual considerations are often ignored in the rush to achieve results in setting standards in a competitive environment. The suggestion that it may be wise to get clear about concepts before rushing headlong into actions supposedly guided by them may be dismissed as too 'philosophical' an approach. Indeed it is! However, this is seen as a merit rather than a criticism of this book. As Lyas has written, 'no discipline worth bothering about can seek to evade such conceptual enquiries. For first, these enquiries constitute the hygiene of the reasoning of a discipline. Without them we are prey to the loose, the ambiguous, and the down-right slovenly' (Lyas, 1993, p. 156). Accounting regulation stands in need of a little 'hygiene'.

Before that can be done there is the need for a little 'hygiene' in respect to the notion of 'conceptual enquiries'. In modern philosophy the idea of a concept is equated with the *meanings of words* (Craig, 2005, p. 135). An enquiry into concepts is thus an enquiry into the meaning of words or expressions. Three kinds of conceptual enquiry can be identified: descriptive, evaluative and prescriptive conceptual enquiry (Dennis, 2008, pp. 261–263). Wittgenstein suggests that 'the meaning of a word is what is explained by the explanation of the meaning' (Wittgenstein, 1953, §560). The explanation of the meaning of a word is something that gives a rule for the use of the word (Baker and Hacker, 1980, p. 35). One objective of conceptual enquiry is thus to identify the rules for the use of words or expressions that are followed by those who use these expressions. Descriptive conceptual enquiries examine the use of expressions and the explanations that are actually given of their meaning. Wittgenstein claims that 'philosophical problems arise when language *goes on holiday*' (Wittgenstein, 1953, §38). This occurs when there is a misunderstanding of the meaning of words or expressions employed in discourse in a discipline. The extent to which the concepts employed in the discipline of accounting regulation are misunderstood is examined in descriptive conceptual enquiries.

Wittgenstein adopted what has been called a 'naturalistic' view of language. This is the idea that language 'develops over millennia to fit our needs. As something arises that we need to mark off, so we develop, by a linguistic reflex, as it were . . . to mark distinctions that it seemed important to us to make'. It follows that 'to understand the meaning of any term is to understand those human interests, needs and practices in the context of which it arose and into which it fits' (Lyas, 1993, p. 163). One implication of this approach is that concepts are *created* and do not just happen. To understand why a concept has been created for use in a discipline, why a certain meaning or rule for the use of the expression has been established and followed, it is important to grasp the 'human interests, needs and practices'—interests, in short—which constitute the objectives or desires that prompted its creation. This is the role of an evaluative conceptual enquiry. The idea that concepts are created is a key assumption made in the literature on the *social construction of reality*. This has been expressed in the accounting literature as the idea that the concepts we use are shaped by us and not found in nature (Young, 2006, p. 581). An evaluative conceptual enquiry seeks to understand these interests and the beliefs that underpin the creation of the concepts used in a discipline. These constitute the reasons for constructing the concept. Where the descriptive conceptual enquiry identifies different explanations of the meaning of expressions or where the explanations are understood differently this may be because the underlying interests that prompt the development of the concept are different.

A further kind of conceptual enquiry is a prescriptive conceptual enquiry. The objective of such an enquiry is to consider whether, if the explanations of the meaning of an expression suggest the expression is vague and if there appear to be different interests underlying the use of a concept, the concept is actually useful. It considers whether it might be better to adopt one or other of the meanings identified or to abandon the use of the expression entirely where it generates confusion that cannot be cleared up. Where there is evidence that confusion has arisen as a result of misunderstanding our language, where there is evidence that language has 'gone on holiday', then the aim of philosophy is to investigate such lapses with a view to unravelling the knots in our thinking (Baker and Hacker, 1980, p. 288). One way to do this is to see how the concepts relate to underlying desires and beliefs and ensure that differences in understandings about how the concepts can fulfil them are cleared up. This is a justification for prescriptive conceptual enquiries. The book employs these three methods in examining the nature of accounting regulation.

2 The Nature of Modern Accounting Practice

In considering the nature of modern accounting practice it seems sensible to start with the question 'What is accounting?' A blindingly obvious answer is that accounting and financial reporting are things accountants *do*. This answer provides a key to understanding what goes on when accountants undertake accounting—namely, they perform actions. It also makes us think about both *what* they are doing in doing accounting and also to consider *why* they are doing what they are doing. Many textbooks on accounting begin by considering the question 'What is accounting?' An answer may be given by quoting the American Institute of Accountant's (now AICPA, American Institute of Certified Public Accountants) definition of accounting as 'the art of recording, classifying, and summarizing, in a significant manner and in terms of money, transactions and events which are in part at least, of a financial character, and interpreting the results thereof' (AICPA, 1941, quoted in Berry, 1993, p. 2). The AICPA Accounting Principles Board (APB) define accounting as 'a service activity'. The American Accounting Association describe accounting as 'the process of identifying, measuring and communicating economic information to permit informed judgments and decisions by the users of the information' (quoted in Kam, 1990, pp. 33–34). What is explicit in the APB definition and implicit in the other descriptions of what accounting is about is that accounting is an *activity* or *action*. Recording, classifying, summarizing, measuring and communicating are all examples of things accountants *do*. What is also obvious is that the actions involved are *intentional*. They are not accidental, for those undertaking them *intend* to perform them.

INTENTIONAL ACTIONS

The analysis of intentional actions in the philosophical literature is complex, and this is not the place for a full analysis of such actions. In some sense, intentional actions are actions that we *want* to do (Goldman, 1970, p. 50). It has also been suggested that wanting to do something *causes* us to do it (Goldman, 1970, p. 93). If one performs an action *because* one wanted to perform it the 'because' may indicate a *causal* explanation. The desire to act is part of the causal explanation of the action. If we do something intentionally then we want to do it, and having such a desire caused the action to occur. There is another strand of thought in the philosophical literature that says that intentional actions 'are the actions to which a certain sense of the question "Why?" is given application; the sense is of course that in which the answer, if positive, gives a reason for acting' (Anscombe, 1957, p. 9). To take a common, or garden, example of an intentional action, consider the action of going to the shop. If the question 'Why did you go to the shop?' is asked then you may mention as a reason a desire to allay hunger and a belief that going to the shop would allow you to buy food which would allay your hunger. Even where one did something solely because one wanted to without any other reason the question is, at least, 'given application' in the sense that the question is not rejected. One does not reply, 'I didn't want to go to the shop' (but went by mistake, say) (Anscombe, 1957, p. 30). For many of the intentional actions that we undertake we can give *reasons* for wanting to perform them. This does not imply that in all cases reasons will be given for actions. Some intentional actions may be performed just because one wanted to perform them.

Although acting because one wants to act in a particular way may be part of a causal explanation of an event, saying that one acted because one has reasons for acting is not a causal explanation. There is a huge philosophical literature on whether reasons are causes of action (see a summary in Goldman, 1973, pp. 76–80). This issue cannot be gone into here. Suffice it to say that there is nothing contradictory in accepting that wanting to do something causes one to do it whilst rejecting the view that having a reason for wanting to do something is a causal explanation of doing it. Having reasons for an action may not be the kind of event or state of affairs that lends itself to use in causal explanations.

Even though someone may not put forward reasons for wanting to perform an action, if they *decide* to perform an intentional action then they *must* have reasons for wanting to perform it. This is because, *as a matter of meaning*, deciding to perform an intentional action—that is, decision-making—*is* coming to have a desire to act *as a result of reasoning*. This does not preclude coming to have a desire to act as a result of something else, but then this would not count as making a decision. Decision-making and reasoning go together, and, hence, if one wants to understand what is involved in making a decision one has to understand the reasoning involved. One may want to perform an action without deciding one wants to do so. The action which follows from this desire is intentional, but one has not decided to perform it. If one has decided to do something then it does not make sense to say that one does not have reasons for wanting to perform it. Wittgenstein suggests that the concept of a reason is related to that of *reasoning* (Hacker, 1996, p. 58). In other words, one cannot talk about having reasons unless there has been reasoning of some kind. Actions that are the result of decision-making are intentional actions for which reasons for wanting to perform them can be given. This throws light on the literature of decision-making, for to explore decision-making is to explore the reasoning involved in coming to want to perform an intentional action. The process of decision-making is the process of reasoning. To understand decision-making is thus to grasp the kind of reasoning involved. Reasoning to intentional actions is often referred to in the philosophical literature as 'practical reasoning'.

PRACTICAL REASONING

In the accounting literature practical reasoning is sometimes referred to as 'means-end' reasoning (Archer, 1993) or 'instrumental' reasoning (Mattessich, 1995). There are two kinds of premise that appear in such reasoning. The first kind of premise expresses a *desire to do something to bring about a certain end or objective*. It is not the kind of intense or emotion-laden desire sometimes implied when one talks about a desire. It simply means being 'inclined toward' something or 'feeling favourably' towards it (Goldman, 1970, p. 49). One important characteristic of these desires is that they are not the expression of an *idle wish* or *hope* that something will come about. They express a desire *to do something*—that is, *to perform an action*—that will bring about a certain end or objective or fulfilment of a desire one wants to bring about (Anscombe, 1957, §35). The first kind of premise might be described as indicating the 'end' in the idea of 'means-end' reasoning. Practical reasoning also includes another kind of premise that expresses a *belief* to the effect that the action in question will fulfil the desire. These might be described as the 'means' in 'means-end' reasoning. One needs to determine what one has to do in order to bring about what is desired.

If the action is performed then the desires and beliefs are called the *reason* the agent performed the action (Davidson, 1980, p. 4). A 'reason rationalizes an action if it leads us to see something the agent saw, or thought he saw, in his action—some feature, consequence, or aspect of the action the agent wanted, desired, prized, held dear, thought dutiful, beneficial, obligatory, or agreeable' (Davidson, 1980, p. 3). The conclusion of the reasoning from such premises is sometimes characterised as an action. However, it is more accurate to say that what is concluded is a *desire to perform the action*. The desire to perform intentional actions is explained by citing the reasons for actions. As a result of wanting to do something, the action may be performed. As suggested earlier, this can be explained in terms of a *causal* connection whereby the action that results is *caused* by having the desire to perform it. Where the action is performed the reason for the action is given by citing the reasons identified in the practical reasoning. Intentional actions are purposive in that the reasons for the action mention the purpose of the action—that is, what wanted to be brought about in performing the action. This is sometimes described as the objective or end of the intentional action.

The kind of reasoning to a desire to perform an action would be of the following form:

> I want to do something that will bring about A (A = the end or objective or something that is desired).
> Doing X (X = an action) will bring about A.
> I want to do X.

Having a reason for acting expressed in the practical reasoning thus involves '(a) having some sort of pro attitude toward actions of a certain kind, and (b) believing (or knowing, perceiving, noticing, remembering) that his action is of that kind' (Davidson, 1980, p. 3). The pair is called the *primary reason*, or *reason* for short, why the agent performed the intentional action (Davidson, 1980, p. 4). Understanding the nature of practical reasoning is important, for this determines the kind of premises that are expressed in such reasoning.

WHAT KIND OF REASONING IS PRACTICAL REASONING?

It is important to understand that practical reasoning of this kind is *not* deductive reasoning. The logical form of the reasoning set out in the example of practical reasoning above is A and B, therefore C (where A and B are the premises and C the conclusion of the argument). This is clearly not a *sound* or *valid* form of deductive argument (Lemmon, 1965, pp. 1–5). Deductive reasoning has certain characteristics which must be grasped. If the premises of deductive reasoning are accepted then the conclusion *must* be accepted. With deductive reasoning the content of the conclusion is present, at least implicitly, in the premises, and hence such reasoning is *nonampliative*. If new premises are added to the argument then it remains valid and the conclusion still follows. In other words, it is *erosion-proof*. The validity of a deductive argument is all-or-nothing, for such arguments are totally valid or invalid and the argument does not come in different degrees of strength (for discussion of the characteristics of deductive reasoning see Salmon, 1992, p. 11). These characteristics imply that as long as one accepts the premises then the conclusions follow necessarily. In undertaking such reasoning *no choices or decisions need to be made* and *no judgement needs to be exercised* in drawing a conclusion.

To go back to the common, or garden, example of an intentional action of going to the shop, the reasoning which identifies the reason for acting would be of this form:

> I want to do something to allay hunger.
> I believe that going to the shop will allow me to buy food which would allay my hunger.
> Therefore, I want to go to the shop.

If you subsequently go to the shop, and this is because you want to go, then your reasons for the intentional action of going to the shop are as set out before.

That this reasoning is not deductive can be seen by noting that there is *no necessity* to accept the conclusion given the premises. One may be hungry and accept that going to the shop might allay hunger and yet one may not wish to go to the shop, for one might have more pressing desires. The conclusion is not implicit in the premises but is *ampliative* and goes beyond what is contained in the premises. If you add to these premises that you believe a thug is waiting to kill you at the shop, and you do not want to die, you may conclude you do not want to go to the shop. Such an argument is not *erosion-proof*. The conclusion might be accepted with *different strengths* depending on how much you want what is expressed by the first premise. How much do you want to allay hunger? Do you want it more than you want something else that might require an action at odds with going to the shop?

It would be possible to make the argument deductive by recasting it as the following:

> If I want to do something to allay hunger and believe that going to the shop will allow me to buy food which would allay my hunger then I want to go to the shop.
> I want to do something to allay hunger and believe that going to the shop will allow me to buy food which would allay my hunger.
> Therefore, I want to go to the shop.

This is a good deductive argument of the form 'if A then B', 'A', therefore B. However, the first premise is simply a re-expression of the original practical reasoning. If there is doubt about accepting the conclusion given the premises then there is doubt about accepting the first premise. Both the original argument, and hence the new premise, may not be acceptable given the problem that performing the action in question might lead to one's death. It would be difficult to formulate conditionals that one would accept in all cases regardless of the other consequences acceptance might have.

Other stratagems might be adopted to try and make practical reasoning deductive. One suggestion might be as such:

> I always want to do something that will allay my hunger.
> I believe that going to shop will allow me to buy food which would allay my hunger.
> Therefore, I want to go to the shop.

The first premise blocks the possibility that, on this occasion, one wants something else more than one wants to do something to bring about A. If one *always* wants it then one wants it on this occasion regardless of whatever else one wants. One problem with a premise of the kind 'I always want . . . ' is that, if taken literally, such a premise is insane (Anscombe, 1957, §33). What it means is that one *always* has to be looking around for actions that fulfil the desire. This kind of monomania would not be accepted by any sane person. Such a premise would normally be modified by some indication of the context in which the desire is to be fulfilled. Something along the lines of 'whenever I am in a situation where I am hungry and can allay it easily then I always want to allay my hunger' would be more acceptable. The second premise would then be altered to say, 'I am hungry and believe going to the shop can be done easily and will allow me to buy food to allay my hunger'. Once again, the first premise is unlikely to be acceptable. Would one want to go to the shop even if it was easy to accomplish if a murderer was known to be lying in wait? Would the premise have to be further modified to exclude this situation? What if there were other circumstances that would preclude its acceptability? Could a premise be formulated that would exclude all such circumstances?

Another problem arises with the second part of the premise. It says that one always wants to do *something* to allay hunger. What if there were lots of ways to allay hunger—going to a restaurant, canteen, soup kitchen, and so on? Although one wants to do *something*, one may have to decide which of the different actions that result in allaying hunger are to be performed. There is no *necessity* in accepting *any one* of them even if there is the necessity of accepting *at least one* of them. This means that a *choice* or *decision* needs to be made in drawing the conclusion that one wants to perform a certain action, for the argument does not necessitate that one particular action be performed. This suggests that reasoning with such a premise cannot be deductive since a conclusion to perform a particular action, say of going to the shop, is not necessitated by the premises. One could overcome this problem by rephrasing the first premise as 'I always want to do anything/ everything that will allay my hunger', but this would lead to the kind of insanity warned about earlier, even if modified by statements about the ease of performing the action. Do you really mean 'anything/everything'? What if you have to kill, which may be easy to do if you have a suitable weapon, to get to the shop?

The problem with trying to make practical reasoning deductive in these ways is that it is difficult to accept the kinds of premises that would be required. The premises that were introduced earlier involved *universal* expressions such as 'always' or 'anything' or 'everything'. In other words, the desires that are expressed in the first premise involve some kind of *generality*. They are not wanted on one occasion but more generally. With reasoning to actions in everyday life that start with the desire 'I want to do something that will bring about *A*' there is no suggestion that what is wanted is wanted on any other occasion than the present one. The reasoning involved is not deductive.

Some philosophers appear to argue that if the reasoning involved in identifying reasons for either actions or events is not deductive then it is defective.

An example of this is in relation to inductive reasoning. Thus Popper (1963) argues that because inductive reasoning is not deductive then it should not be used in science. Scientists should formulate conjectures and use deductive reasoning to derive implications for experience that may falsify them. The processes of formulating hypotheses are not rational, so if induction is used, so much the worse for them. Obviously, a full examination of these arguments is not within the scope of this work. It is worth pointing out that philosophers such as Wittgenstein have suggested that reasoning that is not deductive may still be acceptable. He argues that the attempt to justify induction was pointless. As he puts it, 'from childhood up I learnt to judge like this. *This is* judging.' (Wittgenstein, 1969, §§128–129). This is 'the framework within which we learn to give reasons for doing and believing' (Hacker, 1996, p. 64). Given that the concept of reason is related to that of reasoning, the reasons we have depend upon the kind of reasoning we accept as valid. If we accept inductive reasoning as valid then the premises in the reasoning constitute reasons for believing the conclusion. It does not follow that something can only count as a reason if it is expressed in reasoning that is deductive. If inductive and practical reasoning are not deductive, this does not rule them out as invalid kinds of reasoning if they are used in science and in everyday life. What kinds of reasoning and premises are involved when the actions to be performed are the intentional actions of accounting?

THE INTENTIONAL ACTIONS OF ACCOUNTING

If accountants are performing intentional actions of accounting then they must want to perform them. If asked *why* they want to do so they may give reasons for such actions. To simplify matters, we will consider only acts that constitute accounting and financial reporting rather than those that count as management accounting. We will call these actions 'accounting' for short. If accountants are asked why they want to perform such actions they may give a variety of answers. They might say that they want to make a living and believe that by performing these actions this will be achieved. This is probably a truthful answer but, perhaps, is not the kind of answer that would be expected of a *professional*. What is expected of professionals is that they want to achieve something that they, as a group, have agreed to be the objectives or ends of their activities. The interlocutor may well have taken for granted that the person questioned performed such actions to make a living, but the reason they were looking for was something other than this kind of self-interested motivation. It is taken for granted that there is some such motivation for accounting, but the questioner is asking for some other *justification* for the way the accounting is done in the circumstances. An answer that mentioned something like the value of accounting to people other than to the accountants performing it—that is, some justification from the perspective of a professional—would be the kind of thing expected. The kind of objective or end which is expected to underlie accounting actions might be something like the answer given by the AAA quoted earlier, which states that the purpose of accounting is 'to permit informed judgments and decisions by the users of the information'. More explicitly, APB No. 4 states that the function of accounting is 'to provide quantitative information, primarily financial in nature, about economic entities that is intended to be useful in making economic decisions, in making reasoned choices among alternative courses of action' (APB, 1970). A more up-to-date take on this subject is given in the revised International Accounting Standards Board/ Financial Accounting Standards Board (IASB/FASB) conceptual framework, which states that 'the objective of general purpose financial reporting is to provide financial information about the reporting entity that is useful to existing and potential investors, lenders and other creditors in making decisions about providing resources to the entity' (IASB, 2010, OB2). These statements express *what is wanted from accounting actions* whereby such actions are seen as those of a professional other than to achieve certain self-interested desires.

All these reasons would appear as premises in practical reasoning to a particular accounting action. They suggest that the person undertaking the action wanted to achieve an end of this kind through the action of accounting and believed the action in question would achieve it. Accounting actions are desired in order to achieve wanted ends or objectives. Desires of this kind could be expressed as a premise in practical reasoning such as, 'I want to do something that will provide financial information about the reporting entity that is useful to existing and potential investors, lenders and other creditors in making decisions about providing resources to the entity'. The accountant would then look around for an action they believe would fulfil this objective. The accounting action desired as a conclusion to the reasoning is the one that is believed will fulfil this desire. It is thus possible to see that the statement of objectives in the conceptual framework expresses a desire premise of this kind that is to be used in practical reasoning to accounting actions. This kind of reasoning might also be called 'rational calculation', which sees 'decisions as based on an evaluation of alternatives in terms of their consequences for preferences'—that is, it is a 'logic of consequences' (March, 1994, p. 57). One determines what one wants, looks around for actions that will fulfil what one desires and then one concludes that one wants to perform the act that will fulfil them. Although this might be referred to as a 'logic of consequences' and 'rational calculation', the reasoning involved is practical reasoning and the logic is whatever kind of logic is involved in reasoning of this kind.

Practical reasoning of this kind looks odd, though. Do accountants reason like this when they decide to undertake particular accounting actions? It would be rather time consuming if accountants were to consider, in each particular reporting situation, what they wanted to bring about through their actions and their beliefs about what actions would bring about these ends. They might instead decide *in advance* what is to be done in certain *kinds* of circumstances—that is, what to do *in general* in such circumstances. In other words, they adopt a premise in reasoning to actions of the kind 'I always want to do X in circumstance Y'. If they believe that 'this is circumstance Y' then they will conclude 'I want to do X'. Deciding what to do in advance in certain kinds of circumstance—that is, wanting to do something in general—constitutes *reasoning to the adoption of a rule*. Adopting a rule is also an intentional action that is undertaken for reasons. Other intentional actions follow from this action, and the reason for undertaking these other actions, as is considered in the following, is that a rule has been adopted. What this suggests is that although one decides to adopt a rule, having adopted it there is some abrogation of decision-making in the future. The rule may, in some sense, *bind* one to act in a certain way. Rawls talks about 'the abdication of full liberty to act on utilitarian and prudential grounds' (Rawls, 1955, p. 162) or, it might be added, on other grounds, where certain kinds of rules are adopted. That we 'must' do something, as Wittgenstein says, 'corresponds to the inexorability of our attitude towards our techniques' (from his *Zettel*, §299, quoted in Baker and Hacker, 1985, p. 269). The necessity of acting in a certain way, given a rule, arises from a *determination* to be *bound* by the rule. The decision to adopt a rule rather than decide what to do in particular situations may be because adopting a rule is thought to be *useful*. Adopting accounting rules may be useful in that accountants then have 'handy rules for our daily work'. Rules of this kind can be seen in the 'accounting manuals of big firms' that ensure consistency in what is done and result in comparability for financial statements produced by following rules (Baxter, 1981, p. 6). If accountants reason to the desire to adopt a rule then the practical reasoning would not start with a premise that expresses what is wanted in particular circumstances but rather about what is wanted *generally* in kinds of financial reporting situations or circumstances. They would then consider beliefs of a *general* kind about what kinds of reporting actions would bring about this objective or end. The conclusion of such reasoning would not be a desire for a *specific* action to be undertaken on a particular occasion but rather a desire to do something in *general*—that is, in these kinds of reporting situation. Accountants may set themselves *rules*, general prescriptions, about what they should do in such situations. This is why rules are characterized as having *generality*.

What is missing from the picture of an individual accountant considering what she wants from an accounting action and what actions she believes will achieve this desire is the fact that accounting is a rule-governed *practice*. It has been suggested that 'accounting rules now exert a dominating influence on the practice of accounting' (West, 2003, p. 66). If accounting actions are actions of following rules then when the question 'Why did you perform accounting action X?' is asked the answer will mention a rule, or, more specifically, the reason for performing the action includes a desire to follow a rule. The claim that accounting rules dominate the practice of accounting is a claim that in explaining or justifying accounting actions, rules are part of the reason for such actions. In order to understand this it is necessary to understand what it is to follow a rule and the nature of rule-governed practices.

WHAT ARE RULES?

The suggestion that in performing an act of accounting the accountant is following a rule needs to be carefully understood. In the accounting context the expression 'rule' is often associated with a particular kind of prescription and is contrasted with another kind of prescription, namely 'principles'. There is a debate as to whether accounting standards should contain rules and be 'rules-based' or whether they should contain principles and be 'principles-based'. The suggestion that accountants are following rules in performing accounting actions is agnostic as to whether the prescriptions are rules or principles. The expression 'rule', as it is used here, is to be understood as it is explained in the legal literature where it is 'a general prescription guiding conduct or action in a given type of situation. A typical rule, in this sense, prescribes that in circumstances X, behaviour of type Y ought, or ought not to be, or may be, indulged in by persons of class Z' (Twining and Miers, 1976, p. 48). It is acknowledged that 'there are many kinds of guidance, and there are many different ways of prescribing'. The expression 'rule' is 'a term for the genus of which precepts, regulations, rules of thumb, conventions, principles, guiding standards and even maxims are examples' (Twining and Miers, 1976, p. 49). The expression 'rule', as it is used here, covers both rules and principles. In the legal context rules have three characteristics:

1. A rule is *prescriptive* (concerned with ought or ought not, may or may not or can or cannot) rather than descriptive (concerned with factual *descriptions* of behaviour).
2. A rule is *general* (concerned with *types* of behaviour in *types* of situations, not with prescriptions governing a single event).
3. A rule guides *behaviour* (that is, activities, acts or omissions) (Twining and Miers, 1976, p. 48).

What is involved in following a rule?

FOLLOWING A RULE

Rules and rule-following are important in the philosophy of Wittgenstein. He undertakes an investigation of language which is conceived as a *rule-governed activity*. This is why he spends some time elucidating the idea of a rule and what is involved in following a rule. His philosophy will help in understanding what is implied by saying that an accountant may be following a rule in performing particular accounting actions. Whether or not someone is following a rule is evident from certain 'background activities' against which the action takes place. These have been referred to as 'normative activities' (Baker and Hacker, 1985, p. 47). A person's action is normative in so far as they are following a rule or are guided by/guide themselves by reference to a rule. This is 'manifest in the manner in which he uses rules, invokes rule-formulations, refers to rules in *explaining* what he did, *justifying* what he did in the face of criticism, *evaluating* what he did and *correcting* what he did, *criticizing* his mistakes, and so forth' (Baker and Hacker, 1985, p. 45). The rule is part of the *reason* he gives for wanting to perform the actions he is performing (Baker and Hacker, 1985, p. 156). In other words, the purpose or objective of doing what is intentionally done is that the person performing the act *wants to follow the rule* and believes the action in question is *in accord with the rule*. The reasons for an accounting action of following rules that are set out in practical reasoning include a premise that states a *desire* to follow a rule and a *belief* that what the accountant was doing was in accord with the rule. Where accounting action is explained, justified, evaluated, corrected or criticized by reference to rules then accounting is an activity of following rules.

Whether or not accountants are following rules is an empirical question that can only be answered by invoking empirical evidence of the normative activities of accountants. For example, if an accountant is asked why he wants to perform a particular accounting action of reporting inventory he may give as his reason that he wants to act in accord with the rule in IAS 2: 'report inventory at the lower of cost and net realisable value'. The practical reasoning of an accountant to a desire to act in a certain way would be something like this:

> I want to follow rule X (e.g. State inventories at the lower of cost and net realisable value (IAS 2)).
> I believe that doing A is in accord with rule X (e.g. I believe that the lower of cost and net realisable value for inventories γ in company δ is £5 million).
> Therefore, I want to do A (e.g. State inventories in company δ at £5 million).

If an accountant goes on to state inventories in company δ at £5 million then he would explain, and give as part of his reason for this intentional action, the desire to follow the rule in IAS 2 and the belief that stating inventories at £5 million is in accord with the rule.

In order to fulfil the desire to follow a rule it is necessary to understand *what is in accord with the rule*—that is, to grasp what acts *accord* with it and what acts do not accord with it (Baker and Hacker, 1985, p. 97). As noted earlier, having decided what is to be done in kinds of situations by promulgating a rule, a constraint is put upon the future behaviour of those who follow the rule. If someone has adopted a rule they have decided they want to follow the rule. This means they want to act *in accord with the rule*. In order to do this it is necessary to have an understanding of the rule. This is because 'to be ignorant or mistaken about what acts are in accord with it is to be ignorant or mistaken about what the rule is. To understand a rule is to know what acts accord with it and what violate it' (Baker and Hacker, 1985, p. 97). This is a matter of understanding *the meaning of the expressions that are used to express the rule*. To act in accord with the inventory rule, accountants have to understand the meaning of the expressions 'inventory', 'cost' and 'net realisable value' as well as the other expressions in the rule-formulation. The desire that is the conclusion of such reasoning is a desire to do what is required in order to follow the rule. In order to follow a rule a person has to be master of the technique of applying a rule, and this is manifest in *practice* (Baker and Hacker, 1985, p. 161). There must be an established pattern of behaviour whereby 'a competent practitioner must address the same task in the same way and do what is required' and 'regular behaviour of the right kind is the criterion for the acquisition and persistence of mastery of a technique'. This also requires an intention to conform to the pattern of behaviour, and there must be criteria of correctness that determines whether or not the technique is correctly applied (Baker and Hacker, 1985, pp. 162–163). If a rule is accepted or adopted then the person *wants to act in accord with the rule when the occasion arises*. Accepting the rule is to want to do something *in general*.

West's claim is an empirical claim that would be justified by examining the reasons given for accounting actions. To justify this claim is to show that the reasons for accounting actions involve rules. It has been suggested that there is another kind of 'logic', a 'logic of appropriateness', where 'decision-making is seen as resulting from rule following'. Individuals and organizations 'follow rules or procedures that they see as appropriate to the situation in which they find themselves' (March, 1994, p. 57). In fact, although the reasoning involved in explaining an action of following a rule is still practical reasoning, there are differences in the premises involved in these two kinds of reasoning. If a 'logic of appropriateness' is involved, the reasoning starts with a desire to follow or act in accord with a rule. The second premise states that a particular action is in accord with the rule. The conclusion of the argument is the desire to perform this action. This contrasts with the 'logic of consequences' where the first premise expresses a desire to do something to bring about a certain end or objective that is desired. When one wants to *do something to bring about an end* one must then consider what one has to do to bring about the end. One wants to do something but is not clear what that something is. The second premise in the argument is a belief that a particular action or kind of action will bring about the fulfilment of the desire expressed in the first premise. In both the 'logic of appropriateness' and the 'logic of consequences' the desire in the first premise includes a *variable* whose value has to be determined. In the case of the 'logic of appropriateness' the variable, the something that has to be done, is to act in accord with a rule. This might be expressed as 'I want to do X, where X is an action and X is in accord with a rule'. 'X' is the variable which needs to be given a value. In order to conclude what has to be done one has to grasp what actions are in accord with the rule. In the case of the 'logic of consequences' the variable is given a value by determining what it is that, as a matter of fact, brings about a certain end. One has to grasp what action will bring about the end. This might be expressed as 'I want to do X, where X is an action and X will bring about a certain end'.

The second premise in the 'logic of consequences' is different from the second premise in the 'logic of appropriateness'. Although the latter might appear to express a 'belief' that an action is in accord with a rule, this is not an *empirical* belief about the causal consequences of doing something. The connection between a rule and what actions are in accord with it is called by Wittgenstein an 'internal connection'. This only means it is a connection based on the *meaning of the expressions in the rule-formulation*. The second premise is not an empirical premise but rather a premise that expresses the meaning of expressions. Actions of following rules depend upon a grasp of the meaning of the expressions in the rule-formulation that determine what is in accord with the rule. The variable in the second premise is filled by an explanation of what actions are in accord with the rule.

Whether the practical reasoning involved in explaining or justifying an action follows a 'logic of consequences' or a 'logic of appropriateness', it is important to acknowledge that further questions may be asked of either the desire premise or the belief premise in such reasoning. Where accountants give as a reason for undertaking an action of accounting and mention a desire to do something that will bring about a certain end then further questions can be asked as to *why this end is wanted*. These questions make more or less sense depending upon whether the desire in question is obviously wanted for itself alone or not. If someone answers that the reason they wanted to go to a shop is that they were hungry and wanted something to eat and believed the shop had food then asking the further question 'Why did you want something to eat?' makes little sense. Going to the shop for food *to allay hunger* is an action that has a 'desirability characterisation' that does not invite further questioning (Anscombe, 1957, §37). Other explanations make less sense and invite further questioning. To the question 'Why did you go down to the river bank?' the answer 'I wanted a plate of mud' does invite the question 'Why did you want a plate of mud?' (Anscombe, 1957, §37). When someone gives as a reason for an action the desire to follow a rule then it often makes sense to ask for reasons for wanting to follow the rule. Given West's contention that accounting actions are generally actions of following a rule, the next section will concentrate on exploring the reasons accountants may want to follow rules of accounting. The answer given can be of different kinds depending upon the *kind of practice of following rules* that is adopted.

ADOPTING A PRACTICE OF FOLLOWING A RULE
AND DIFFERENT KINDS OF PRACTICES

Following a rule is a *practice* (Wittgenstein, 1953, §202). A practice involves a regularity in behaviour, an intention to conform to a pattern or behaviour and a stipulation of what procedures are correct where it is possible to distinguish acts that are in conformity with the practice from those that are not (Baker and Hacker, 1985, pp. 161–165). When accountants adopt a practice of following rules they may give different kinds of reason for doing so. They do not always follow rules because the rules are imposed upon them by other persons or bodies. Accountants can give rules or prescriptions *to themselves*. Where this happens the practice of following rules might be characterized as an *individual practice*.

It has been suggested that deciding to adopt a practice of following a rule is an intentional action that involves practical reasoning. As with particular actions, the reasons given for this action might follow a 'logic of consequences' or a 'logic of appropriateness'. The adoption of a practice of following a rule can be justified by explaining the desire to follow a rule by giving preferences, or what is wanted in adopting a practice, along with beliefs that as a consequence of following the rule the preferences or desires will be met. As noted earlier, given that rules are *general prescriptions* that apply to *kinds* of circumstances on a number of occasions, the reasons given must also apply not on only one occasion but on the various occasions when the rule is to be followed. The desires have to be wanted on the numerous occasions where the rule is to be followed, and it must be believed these desires will be met not just on a single occasion but on numerous occasions. In other words, the desire must be something wanted generally, at least on the occasions when the rule applies, and the belief must have a generality in that it is not enough to believe following the rule will achieve the ends on only one occasion but generally. A simple example will make this clear. If one wants, in general, to do something to avoid injuring people while driving and believes following a rule to drive on the left-hand side of this road will achieve this end then one may conclude one wants to follow the rule to drive on the left-hand side of the road. Both the desire and the belief have generality. Following the Highway Code is something to be done *generally*. The practical reasoning can be characterized as follows:

I generally want to avoid injuring people.
I believe that, in general, driving on the left-hand side of the road will
    result in avoiding injuring people.
Therefore, I generally want to drive on the left-hand side of the road.

The conclusion is that one wants to adopt the practice of driving on the left-hand side of the road. These actions have a regularity or pattern that covers numerous occasions and are wanted *generally*. Sometimes one may express the aforementioned conclusion in terms of something generally wanted. Alternatively, one may express the conclusion as 'drive on the left-hand side of the road'. The latter expression looks like one is giving a prescription to oneself. The two are equivalent. Adopting a rule to do *X* is wanting to do *X* generally.

An alternative explanation of why someone wants to follow a rule or adopt a practice can be given in a 'logic of appropriateness'. Specific rules may be derived from *more general* rules that the person adopting the practice of following the specific rule may want to follow. One example of this might be the desire to follow a rule that requires the depreciation of property, plant and equipment because one wants to follow a rule that requires the matching of expenses against revenue. The reasoning goes something like this:

I want to match all expenses against revenue.

The cost of property, plant and equipment is, as a matter of meaning, an expense.

Matching the cost of the asset against revenue means depreciating the asset.

I want to depreciate property, plant and equipment.

The rule of depreciation is *derived* from the general rule of matching. The desire to follow a general rule explains the desire to follow a more specific rule given this kind of practical reasoning. It is important to appreciate the sense in which the rule expressed in the first premise of the argument is more 'general' than the rule expressed in the conclusion of the argument. Although the matching rule implies the depreciation rule, the depreciation rule does not imply the matching rule because, as a matter of meaning, although matching *all* expenses against revenue implies matching a particular expense against revenue, matching a particular expense against revenue does not imply matching *all* expenses against revenue. One rule is more general than another if it implies the other rule but the other does not imply it. Further questions might be asked about why the person concerned wants to follow the general rule. If there is no further rule of an even more general nature then the request for an explanation of the adoption of the practice is a request for an explanation within a 'logic of consequences'.

Justifying the adoption of an individual practice might be said to be a matter of 'theorising' about the rules to be adopted. Given these explanations such 'theorising' may involve considering the ends to be achieved by a practice or considering general rules from which other rules can be derived. These two kinds of 'theorising' give rise to different 'theories'. This will not be explained further in this chapter but will be considered in the next chapter. At the moment is it important to note that not all practices are individual practices. Practices might be *conventional* practices rather than individual ones. These are practices that members of a group conform to and the reason they do so is that they expect the other members to do so and each prefers to do so if the others do so (Blackburn, 1984, p. 120). If a practice is conventional then the practical reasoning that underpins the adopting of a practice of following rules would be as follows:

> I want to act in accord with the requirements I expect others will meet and which I wish to meet if they do so.
> Others are expected to follow the practice of meeting requirements Z.
> I want to adopt the practice of meeting requirements Z.

In such practices, in effect, people want to adopt them because others do so. Practices of this kind may be called 'mimetic processes' (DiMaggio and Powell, 1991, p. 69). There may be various reasons for wanting to do what others do. It may be a response to uncertainty or because it is felt that following the rules that others follow results in success of whatever kind is appropriate (DiMaggio and Powell, 1991, p. 69–70). Whatever the reason, the desire and belief that underpin the desire to adopt a conventional practice are different than in an individual practice.

Not all practices are individual or conventional practices. An *institutional practice* acknowledges the fact that accountants do the same kinds of things because of 'collective rationality' imposed by institutions (DiMaggio and Powell, 1991). This means rules are followed because they are required by an institution whose authority is accepted. Where rules are adopted for this kind of reason the practice of following rules is an *institutional* practice (Dennis, 2010b, p. 140). An example of such a practice would be the practice of accountants following the rules in accounting standards because an institution, the IASB for example, requires them to do so and accountants accept their authority. The kind of reasoning towards the adoption of the practice would look as follows:

> I want to act in accord with the requirements set out by an institution Y.
> Institution Y requires me to meet requirements Z.
> I want to adopt the practice of following the requirements Z.

In the accounting context an example of such reasoning would be the following:

> I want to follow rules that are promulgated by the IASB.
> ISA X is promulgated by the IASB.
> I want to follow ISA X.

It is possible in some jurisdictions that accounting is a *legal practice*. A legal practice might be defined as a practice where rules are followed because they are required by the law (Dennis, 2010b, p. 140). If reasoning is of the following kind then the practice is a legal one. The reasoning would look like this:

> I want to act in accord with the requirements set out by law.
> The law requires me to meet requirements Z.
> I want to adopt the practice of following the requirements Z.

In some jurisdictions accounting rules are included in codes of law and are adopted for reasons of this kind.

This analysis suggests that social practices can be further distinguished into conventional, institutional and legal practices. Social practices are shared practices, but practices can be shared for various reasons that determine further kinds of practices. What identifies social practices as being of one or the other kind are *the reasons given for adopting the practice.* Just as accounting actions are distinguished as rule-governed by the reasons given for undertaking them so rule-governed practices can be identified as practices of a certain kind by the reasons given for adopting the practice of following rules. It is worth considering how accounting practices have changed by considering a very brief history of standard setting which shows how accounting practices have developed into institutional or legal practices.

PRACTICES DETERMINED BY STANDARD SETTERS

Accounting and financial reporting practices today are often institutional or legal practices. It is not always easy to say what kind of practice is operational in particular countries. In the U.S. there is a complex mix of practices. Companies registered with the Securities and Exchange Commission (SEC) have to obey SEC accounting and auditing rules, but the SEC leaves the determination of these rules, with a few exceptions, to the Financial Accounting Standards Board whose pronouncements have substantial authoritative support. For companies not registered with the SEC there is no compulsory audit or published financial accounting, but if the company requires an audit then the Code of Professional Ethics of AICPA requires observation of the rules of the FASB with the penalty of expulsion for failure to do so (Nobes and Parker, 2006, ch. 7). In the European Union (EU) all listed companies must follow the accounting standards issued by the International Accounting Standards Board, as long as they are approved by the European Commission (Alexander, Britton and Jorissen, 2011, ch. 3).

The requirement to follow IASB standards in the UK is a legal one which is dependent upon acceptance of EU law. Hence, for accountants the practice is a legal one. However, the legislature adopts the standards of the IASB largely because they want to promulgate standards that an institution promulgates, which suggests it is an institutional practice from the perspective of the EU. The EU only accepts the rules they think are 'good' rules. This raises the question of why standard setters promulgate rules. Obviously, standard setters would not promulgate rules if they believed no one would follow them. Implicit in their reasons for promulgating particular accounting standards is the belief that by promulgating standards in general, practicing accountants will follow them. Accountants are *required* to follow the rules set out in the law or, in a number of jurisdictions over the world, by standard setters who regulate the practice of accounting. Modern accounting practice is *regulated*. The practice of accounting is an institutional or legal practice, and accountants want to follow the rules promulgated by a legislature or an institution such as a standard setter. Where legislatures adopt the rules of a standard setter it is reasonable for the standard setter to believe that if they promulgate a standard it will be followed. The question 'Why do you want to promulgate rule *X*?' is directed at answering the question of why standard setters bother promulgating rules but is meant to elicit from them reasons they want to promulgate *particular* standards, assuming they will be followed.

The questions of why a legislature or an individual accountant adopts a practice and why an institution promulgates a rule may not always be kept apart. It may be that the legislature or accountant wants to follow the rules established by an institution because they believe the institution promulgates the rule for 'good' reasons. One example of what might be considered a 'good' reason for an institution promulgating a standard would be that the rules in the standard meet certain objectives or ends of accounting such as those that are set out in conceptual frameworks. One purpose of the conceptual framework would be to provide reasons for the standard setter to want to promulgate rules, which convinces a legislature or accountant to adopt them. This might also be expressed as the belief that an institution promulgates rules based on some 'theory' of accounting or financial reporting. In the next chapter we will consider the nature of 'theories' of accounting of this kind and also the nature of a conceptual framework. We will not further examine the question of why accountants might adopt rules established by an institution or legislature.

SUMMARY

Intentional actions are those to which a certain sense of the question 'Why?' is given application, the sense in which what is being asked for are reasons for performing the action. Where accountants perform intentional actions they can be asked for reasons for performing the action set out in practical reasoning that has as its conclusion the desire to perform the action in question. The reasons may include a desire to perform an action that will achieve a certain objective, or purpose, that constitutes something the person who performs the action wants to fulfil. The reasons also involve a belief that the action in question will achieve the objective. The conclusion is a desire to act which, if the action results from having such a desire, is performed for the reasons set out in the practical reasoning.

3 The Role of Theory and of Conceptual Frameworks in Standard Setting

It was suggested in the last chapter that where financial accounting and reporting is an institutional practice, or where institutions provide rules of accounting that are adopted in legal practices, then the question 'Why follow the rules of accounting in standards?' can be answered by giving reasons individual accountants or legislatures decide to adopt the rules promulgated by institutions like standard setters. An alternative is to interpret it as a question about why standard setters promulgate the rules that are adopted by accountants or legislatures. Answers to the latter interpretation of the question will be given in this chapter.

When the new conceptual framework project was begun in 2005, the two parties involved, the Financial Accounting Standards Board and the International Accounting Standards Board, stated that 'each Board bases its accounting standards decisions in large part on the foundation of objectives, characteristics, definitions and criteria set forth in their existing conceptual frameworks' (FASB/IASB, 2005, p. 1). The goal of the project is convergence of the frameworks into 'a common framework that both Boards can use in developing new and revised accounting standards' (FASB/IASB, 2005, p. 1). In SFAC 8 the FASB acknowledge that 'the Board itself is likely to be the most direct beneficiary of the guidance by Concepts Statements. They will guide the Board in developing accounting and reporting guidance by providing the Board with a common foundation and basic reasoning on which to consider merits of alternatives' (FASB, 2010, SFAC 8). The objective of the IASB conceptual framework is 'to facilitate the consistent and logical formulation of IFRSs. The *Conceptual Framework* also provides a basis for the use of judgement in resolving accounting issues' (IASB, 2010, Preface, §8). This kind of purpose was also implied in the introduction to the UK's *Statement of Principles for Financial Reporting* (ASB, 1999) where it was stated that 'the primary purpose of articulating such principles is to provide a coherent frame of reference to be used by the Board in the development and review of accounting standards . . . As such it will play an important role in the development of accounting standards' (ASB, 1999, §§2–3). It goes on to say that 'a set of high-level principles' is 'designed to help in setting standards' (ASB, 1999, §13). The ASB's 'principles' are equivalent to the FASB's 'concepts'. The fact that standards are developed using the conceptual framework is one of the meanings implied by the statement that such standards are 'principles-based' or 'concepts-based' (Schipper, 2003, p. 62; Tweedie, reported in FASB, 2002, p. 4). The implication of all these statements is that one important purpose of the conceptual framework is to play a role in decision-making, in particular in assisting standard setters in making *rational decisions* about which accounting standards to promulgate.

The conception of a conceptual framework emerged as something that assists in making rational standard setting decisions developed in a context where the science of decision was acknowledged as increasingly important. Decision-making required the recognition of a problem, the specification of the goals or objectives that would 'define an optimal solution' to the problem, consideration of all the possible alternatives and selection of the alternative that 'maximised the likelihood of achieving the desired goal' (Young, 2006, p. 585). From this perspective a conceptual framework is something that specifies the goals or objectives that define an optimal solution to standard setting problems identified by standard setters and is to be used by them to consider alternatives and propose a solution—that is, an accounting standard—meant to maximize these goals or objectives. In order to understand how a conceptual framework can assist in making decisions the process of decision-making and the nature of the rationality involved must be grasped. It was suggested in the previous chapter that understanding rational decisions is a matter of understanding the kind of reasoning involved in making such decisions and the nature of the premises and conclusions of such reasoning. This will throw light on the nature of a conceptual framework as something that assists standard setters in rational decision-making.

STANDARD SETTING DECISIONS AS INTENTIONAL ACTIONS

The most useful place to start in understanding the nature of a conceptual framework, as it was in understanding the nature of accounting, is with the idea that standard setting is an *intentional action* performed by standard setters like the FASB or IASB. Standard setting is not an *event* which needs to be explained using the kinds of methods used to explain events in science. It is an intentional action that is done for reasons. The connection of the conceptual framework with reasons and reasoning is well understood, as the aforementioned quote from SFAC 8 makes clear.

There are a range of possible answers to the question 'Why do you want to promulgate rule *X*?' when asked of standard setters. The 'official' answer that the IASB and the FASB give to such a question can be seen in the quote from the two boards provided at the beginning of the chapter. A conceptual framework is used in reasoning towards the desire to promulgate accounting standards. In this sense it is *rational*, for decisions are taken for reasons that are understood in connection with some kind of reasoning. That the conceptual framework is used in this way is maintained by standard setters themselves, for example by a member of the IASB, Mary Barth (Barth, 2007, p. 7). Against this are statements by sceptics such as Dopuch and Sunder, who claim 'there is little evidence that official statements of objectives of financial accounting have had any direct effect on the determination of financial accounting standard' (Dopuch and Sunder, 1980, p. 18). Their claim was made relatively soon after the publication of the first chapter of the U.S. conceptual framework, *Statement of Financial Accounting Concepts No. 1* (SFAC 1), and their 'initial guess' was that the objectives in SFAC 1 'will be ignored in future rule-making activities, just as were those from previous authoritative attempts. Following the publication of these objectives, the Board will probably feel obliged to pay lip service to them in its future pronouncements, but these pronouncements will not be affected in any substantive way by what is contained in the present documents' (Dopuch and Sunder, 1980, p. 18). It is not easy to determine whether standard setters are paying only 'lip service' to the conceptual framework or whether one should take their claims at face value. Given the prediction of Dopuch and Sunder, it is easy to say of standard setters, 'They would say that, wouldn't they?'

There is a large literature on the political nature of standard setting. Zeff defines 'political' to mean 'self-interested considerations or pleadings by preparers and others that may be detrimental to the interests of investors and other users' (Zeff, 2002, p. 43). Numerous examples of standard setting decisions that appear to be prompted by political considerations have been given (Watts and Zimmerman, 1978; Solomons, 1978; Hines, 1989; Zeff, 2002). The claim that standard setters do not make standard setting decisions based upon the principles in a conceptual framework but rather based on political considerations is an argument about the reasons standard setters have for making standard setting decisions. Conceptual frameworks are sometimes justified on the basis that they enable standard setters to resist political pressures on the standard setting process (FASB, 1974). Standards based on reasons given in a conceptual framework are not supposed to be based on reasons that include political considerations. One problem that has been suggested is that existing frameworks do not provide 'a body of knowledge unequivocally to predicate consistent and complete accounting standards' and that such frameworks are a 'technical' and 'functional' failure (Hines, 1989, p. 81). It has also been suggested that conceptual frameworks are themselves the outcome of a political process and therefore constitute 'a set of political declarations expressed in the form of an accounting theory' (Miller, 1990, p. 23). The idea is that standard setting decisions can scarcely be based on the principles in a conceptual framework if those principles do not, actually, constitute reasons for deciding upon such standards. A study of actual standard setting decisions and the reasons for them would be a major work in itself and cannot be attempted here. Instead, some insight into whether it is at least *possible* that conceptual frameworks have been used to make standard setting decisions can be given by examining the kinds of reasoning and reasons that might be used by standard setters in making such decisions. This could then be used to question standard setters about why they have promulgated the standards they have and to assess the reasons and the reasoning they claim to have used.

The idea that the conceptual framework is itself a political statement will not be explored here. A distinction may be drawn between a framework adopted for political reasons and one used to make standard setting decisions. Although the first may be adopted out of self-interest it does not follow that decisions in accordance with the framework are themselves all and only motivated by self-interest. Adopting principles or rules puts constraints upon what can be decided in the future. Although adopting such prescriptions may be motivated by self-interest, making decisions based on such frameworks may not be so motivated unless it can be shown that in accepting a framework of this kind it is possible to foresee all the decisions that will be made using this framework and that these are always in the interest of those adopting the framework. This issue will not be further explored. Instead the role of conceptual frameworks in giving reasons for promulgating standards will be explored.

There are two kinds of answer to the question asked of standard setters— 'Why do you want to promulgate rule X?'—that mirror the two kinds of answer that might be given by individuals who decide to adopt a rule as was considered in the previous chapter. One answer might be that standard setters want to promulgate particular rules that are derived from some more general rule. This is to justify the particular rule by using a 'logic of appropriateness'. The reason for promulgating the specific rule is that standard setters want accountants to act in accord with rules derived from a more general rule, and they believe the specific rule is so derived. It was suggested in the previous chapter that one rule is more general than another if it implies the other rule but the other does not imply it. If the standard setter wants to promulgate rules in standards that are derived from general rules then it would be useful if a conceptual framework set out the general rules to be used in reasoning to a desire to promulgate particular standards. This conception of a conceptual framework, or one kind of theory of accounting, as something that sets out general rules of accounting appears to hark back to a conception of accounting theory that was supplanted when the decision-usefulness approach to theorising became dominant.

ACCOUNTING THEORY AS A SYSTEM OF GENERAL RULES

The kind of theory in vogue before the emergence of the decision-usefulness approach was a theory that has been said to set out 'what accountants do' (Young, 2006). 'Appropriate' accounting practices were 'those that adhered to desirable accounting conventions such as conservatism, consistency, historical cost and matching', and 'official' definitions exhibited 'circular reasoning in that accounting is defined in terms of what accountants do. Accounting methods are justified based upon accounting activities including recording, classifying, and interpreting or upon its conventions such as matching or conservatism' (Young, 2006, p. 582). This appears to confuse two roles for a 'theory' of accounting. The first objective of theories is to *describe* the activity the 'theory' is a theory *about*. This involves defining the subject matter in terms of the activities undertaken. There is nothing circular in defining 'accounting' as 'what accountants do'. This is a form of explanation of the meaning of an expression that, as Wittgenstein points out, is a perfectly serviceable form of explanation (Baker and Hacker, 1980, pp. 36–41). It may be useful as long as those who make use of such a definition know what it is that accountants do. However, it does not, and is not meant to, *justify* accounting practice. It simply re-describes accounting practice and enables someone to move from a statement that someone is accounting to a statement that someone is doing something like recording, classifying and interpreting or vice versa. This provides an answer to the question 'What is accounting?'

Another role for 'theory' is to *justify* these activities. This provides an answer to the question 'Why do you (an accountant) undertake activities X, Y and Z?' Accountants may give as their reason for undertaking the activities of recording, classifying, interpreting and so forth the fact that 'I am an accountant and it is my job to perform accounting activities'. The full answer would be, 'I want to do what my employer requires me to do' and 'I believe that my employer requires me to record, classify, interpret, etc.' Another answer might be 'because such activities are useful', or more fully, 'I want to do what is useful' and 'I believe that recording, classifying, interpreting, etc. is useful'. These answers are given within a 'logic of consequences' where an accountant is expected to justify her actions by mentioning some desire the action in question is supposed to achieve and a belief that performing the action will fulfil this desire.

The reference to accounting conventions in justifying accounting appears to invoke another kind of justification that involves a rule. Particular accounting actions can be justified by invoking a rule. An answer to the question 'Why are you charging a depreciation expense of £5,000?' might be answered by explaining that the accountant wants to follow a rule that requires the depreciation of property, plant and equipment and believes that the rule requires that £5,000 is charged as a depreciation expense. This is to give an explanation within a 'logic of appropriateness'. However, they may go on to explain that they want to follow this rule by saying it is derived from a more general rule of matching, as in the previous chapter. The more general rule can be expressed as 'match against revenue the expenses incurred in earning that revenue' (Alexander, Britton and Jorissen, 2011, p. 13). Other conventions can be similarly expressed as general rules. The prudence convention might be expressed as 'recognise all possible losses, but do not anticipate possible gains' (adapted from Alexander, Britton and Jorissen, 2011, p. 11).

This kind of answer may be given where the practice of accounting is an individual practice and the accountant is required to justify his adoption of a rule. However, where accounting is an institutional one then the reason that might be given for an action is that the depreciation rule is required by an institution and the accountant wants to do what the institution requires. As suggested in the previous chapter, any further questions about why the rule of depreciation is followed—that is, where there is a request for justification of the rule—should be addressed to the institution. The question is really about *why they want to promulgate a depreciation rule*. The answer the institution might give is that the specific rule of depreciation is derived from the more general rule of matching and that they want to promulgate rules that are derived from the more general rule. A theory of accounting that set out the conventions that underpin standard setting decisions would be one that set out general rules to be used in deriving more specific rules of accounting. In effect, Young is arguing that a theory of accounting that operated before the onset of the decision-usefulness approach was one that set out conventions, or general rules, of this kind.

One problem with conventions is that they may be used to derive different rules for accounting for particular items that may be inconsistent or contradictory. These kinds of clashes are well known in the literature. Prudence may conflict with going concern or with matching (Alexander, Britton and Jorissen, 2011, p. 14). This may be one of the reasons this kind of approach to theory fell out of favour and the decision-usefulness approach was adopted in theorising about accounting (Young, 2006). It is worth thinking why these clashes are problematic. If a rule is something one has to follow on *all* occasions when the circumstances for following it arise and if specific rules are to be *deduced* from general ones, the fact that the general rules expressed in conventions lead to inconsistent specific rules means the general rules must themselves be inconsistent. This follows from the nature of deductive reasoning. With such reasoning 'given two valid deductions with incompatible conclusions, their premises must also be incompatible' (Salmon, 1992, p. 26). The sense in which two rules derived from conventions are 'incompatible' is that one cannot follow both of them. To adopt a rule is to want to do something in accord with the rule. If you want to do something in accord with rule X but this means doing something that is not in accord with rule Y, which one also wants to act in accord with, then you cannot want to do something that is in accord with both rule X and rule Y. These rules are inconsistent or incompatible. The general rules must also be inconsistent or incompatible. This is precisely what happens where there are clashes of conventions. At least one of the conventions must be given up. Clashes of this kind may be one of the reasons the convention of prudence has been given up in the revised conceptual framework and no longer appears (Hoogervorst, 2012).

There are two assumptions that underlie the application of conventions in accounting. The first is that conventions are general rules that are to be followed on all occasions when the circumstances for their application exist. In other words, if one adopts a rule, one wants to act in accord with it on all occasions. The second is that general rules are used to deduce more specific rules. Both these assumptions can be challenged. The first assumption is an assumption about the conception of rules. It has been suggested in the legal literature that there are, in fact, two conceptions of rules. This will now be examined.

TWO CONCEPTIONS OF RULES

In the legal literature there is an argument that there are two conceptions of rules (Rawls, 1955). On one conception, a rule is something that has to be followed on *all* occasions when it applies. This is to view rules on the 'practice' conception (Rawls, 1955, p. 162). With this conception of a rule the intention in promulgating a rule is to establish a practice which 'necessarily involves the abdication of full liberty to act on utilitarian and prudential grounds' (Rawls, 1955, p. 162). If standard setters conceive of rules in this way then in following a rule they do not need to consider whether following the rule on a particular occasion will or will not achieve the ends for which it was accepted. The rule, if accepted, will be followed on *all* occasions where it is required and not only on those occasions where following it will achieve these ends. The rule is not to be overridden. Once the rule is accepted there is no further decision to be made, and there is no need for any choice or decision about what is to be done. Judgement does not have to be exercised as to whether or not to do what the rule requires. When one accepts such a rule, one *always wants* to act in accord with it. For example, if an individual accountant adopts the matching principle and conceives of the general rule as on the 'practice' conception (Rawls, 1955, p. 162) then the reasoning to a desire to act in accordance with the rule might be expressed as the following:

> I always want to match expenses with revenue.
> Charging depreciation in financial statements is matching the expense of using an asset to revenue generated by the use of the asset.
> I want to charge depreciation in financial statements/adopt a rule to charge depreciation in financial statements.

The action of charging depreciation is an intentional action performed for reasons that include a desire to follow a general rule of matching and a premise that states that a particular action is, as a matter of meaning, an instance of the matching rule. It is also possible to adopt another rule, the rule that requires charging depreciation, on the basis of accepting the more general rule of matching. Clearly, if you accept one rule on the basis of another then this rule can be used in reasoning to particular actions. Drawing the conclusion that one wants to perform an action or to accept a more specific rule would appear to be a matter of deduction. If you always want to do something and a particular action or rule of action is an instance of doing that thing then one wants to do it or follow the more specific rule. However, if the rule of charging depreciation is not an instance of the prudence rule and one always wants to follow the general rule of prudence then one does not want to charge depreciation or adopt a rule of charging depreciation. There is a conflict. If the reasoning is deductive then one cannot want both general rules, and at least one of the rules must be given up (assuming that the second premises in arguments are acceptable).

There is another conception of rules which takes them as 'rules of thumb' (Rawls, 1955, p. 162). It may be that rules are allowed to be overridden. This is to conceive of rules on the 'summary' conception in that they are 'summaries of past decisions' (Rawls, 1955, p. 158). It may be noted that certain objectives or ends can be achieved by performing certain actions in certain circumstances. A 'rule of thumb' is then adopted whereby certain actions are to be performed in order to achieve these ends. With such rules 'each person is in principle always entitled to reconsider the correctness of a rule and to question whether or not it is proper to follow it in a particular case' (Rawls, 1955, p. 161). To accept such a rule is not to follow it on all occasions but rather to act in accord with it *generally* unless, in particular circumstances, it will not achieve the desired ends. If a rule can be *overridden* then those following the rule must make a choice or a decision as to whether or not to override the rule on each occasion where the rule applies. Rules of this kind require those who follow them to exercise judgement in following them (further discussion of the two conceptions of rules will be found in Dennis, 2010a, pp. 309–310). One way of making this conception of the rule perspicacious is to re-express the rule—the matching rule, for instance—as 'in general I want to match expenses with revenue'. The kind of reasoning to particular actions or rules would look like this:

> In general I want to match expenses with revenue.
> Charging depreciation in financial statements is matching the expense of using an asset to revenue generated by the use of the asset.
> I want to charge depreciation/adopt a rule to charge depreciation in financial statements.

Interestingly, the conclusion does not follow deductively from the premises. One may want to do something in general but may not conclude one wants to do what is generally wanted because, on this occasion, one wants something else. Generally wanting something is compatible with not wanting it on particular occasions. Generally wanting to follow a general rule does not imply deductively that you always want to follow a more specific rule derived from it. In other words, the conclusion one draws in this reasoning does not follow necessarily from the premises. Given the characteristics of deductive reasoning set out in chapter 2, if the premises are true then the conclusion *must* be true and the argument cannot be undermined by the addition of new premises. If one generally wants to follow a rule like matching but adds a premise that one also generally wants to follow a rule like prudence, and then if a specific rule follows matching but not prudence, then one may conclude one does not want to follow the specific rule. With deduction the fact that there are two valid deductions with incompatible conclusions means at least some of the premises must be incompatible. Either prudence or matching has to be rejected. If the reasoning is not deductive then this is not required. One can still want to follow a prudence rule *in general* and a matching rule *in general* even if, on occasions, one cannot follow specific rules derived from them because they are not compatible.

This throws an important light upon how a theory of accounting that involves the identification of conventions might be used to derive more specific rules to be included in accounting standards. If the reasoning is not deductive then the desire to follow a specific rule on the basis of a desire to follow a general rule is not necessitated by acceptance of the general rule. Where there are a number of general rules, introducing another general rule into reasoning which has as its conclusion the desire to follow a specific rule may undermine the conclusion. This does not mean one has to reject one of the general rules. One may still want prudence, in general, and matching, in general. What is distinctive about reasoning that is nondeductive is that some *judgement* needs to be exercised in drawing a conclusion. The conclusion drawn is not necessitated, and so there is some element of choice or decision involved in drawing it. Where a conclusion is drawn some decision or choice may need to be made as to whether to accept a conclusion given the premises or whether one wants to look for other premises that may undermine the argument. This is similar to reasoning from two statistical generalisations where conclusions might be drawn that are incompatible without it being the case that either of the generalisations is untrue (Salmon, 1992, p. 24–26). With reasoning from rules of this kind one is not forced to give up one of the general rules where the conclusions are incompatible. One may decide or choose to do so if there are repeated clashes in using them to draw conclusions, but one does not have to as one would if the reasoning was deductive.

The need to make choices or decisions is what we understand by the exercise of judgement in decision-making. The Canadian Institute of Chartered Accountants (CICA) defined 'judgement' as 'the process of making a choice, a decision, leading to action' (CICA, 1988, p. 4). It was suggested that decision-making involves reasoning to a desire to do something. If the reasoning is not deductive then such reasoning involves choices or decisions that, given the explanation of 'judgement', mean that judgement needs to be exercised in reasoning to a desire to do something—that is, in decision-making. Where general rules of conventions are used to derive specific rules judgement needs to be exercised. The implication is that standard setters who use general rules to derive more specific rules must exercise judgement in reasoning to specific rules.

It is interesting to reflect upon why the idea of identifying conventions in theorising about accounting fell out of favour. If the assumption is that the reasoning from general rules or conventions to specific rules of accounting is deductive then the evidence of clashes between rules derived from different general rules appears to force one to give up at least some of the general rules. For example, standard setters may have been persuaded to give up the concept of prudence and exclude it from a conceptual framework for accounting because of clashes of this kind. It may also have been one reason the approach to theorising that seeks to identify conventions or general rules appears to have lost favour. The search for a 'coherent framework' may be understood as the search from a framework that can be used to *deduce* standard setting decisions. Existing conventions do not appear to provide such a framework (Alexander, Britton and Jorissen, 2011, p. 14).

This discussion suggests that the identification of general rules or conventions may be understood as identifying a framework that can be used to derive specific rules of the kind included in accounting standards where the reasoning involved is not deductive and where deriving the conclusion involves judgement. One meaning of 'principle' in this context might be that it is a convention or general rule used in the derivation of specific rules of accounting. The rejection of this approach may be fuelled by the assumption that decision-making about standards is deductive in nature. What is wanted from a theory of accounting is something that will enable standard setters to deduce standards. The observation that accounting theorising and the project to develop a conceptual framework appear to require the identification of something that can be used to deduce standards has been made many times, and the idea has a long history.

Writing in the nineteenth century, Foster suggested that 'rule-making is a deductive process; given the principles, the rules emerge by logical inference' (quoted in Chambers, 1966, p. 24). Here, 'principles' may mean general rules. Chambers observes that one of the first books on accounting theory, Paton's 1922 book entitled *Accounting Theory*, 'provides one of the earliest promises of the deductive derivation of a set of rules from a *set* of postulates' (Chambers, 1966, p. 25). Littleton's 1953 book *Structure of Accounting Theory* was guided by the idea that 'insofar as there are supporting reasons, it appears that the rules [which accounting theories underpin] are deductively derived' (Chambers, 1966, p. 31). Moonitz, in his Accounting Research Study (ARS) No.1, *The Basic Postulates of Accounting*, stated, 'we are driven to the conclusion, then, that relatively heavy reliance must be placed on deductive reasoning in the development of accounting postulates and principles (Moonitz, 1961, p. 6). Writing much later, Power identifies an underlying assumption that the kind of reasoning that goes on in accounting 'theorising' is thought of as 'either "deductive" or defective' (Power, 1993, p. 48) and draws attention to the FASB conception of a conceptual framework as a 'construct from which accounting standards can be derived deductively' (Power, 1993, p. 55). Again, it has been suggested that 'underlying the entire issue of developing a conceptual framework is the unspoken yet pervasive view of the project's authors that the logical structure for the framework should be a highly deductive one' (Davies, Paterson and Wilson, 1999, p. 81). Mattessich suggests that the term 'normative' as is used in the accounting literature to describe reasoning to rules of accounting of the kind that involves conceptual frameworks is 'synonymous (or at least co-extensive) with "deductive" ' (Archer, 1998, p. 301). What is interesting is that the assumption that what is wanted from theorising is something that can be used to deduce standards has been retained, but the kind of thing involved in such deduction appears to have changed in character. No longer does it appear that such theorising should identify conventions or general rules, but theories of the kind that are constructed in conceptual frameworks involve something different.

It is understandable why there may be a desire for something more in a theory of accounting than simply the identification of general rules or conventions or 'principles' understood in this sense. After all, the next question to be asked about such conventions or general rules is, 'Why do you want to adopt them as general rules or conventions?' The matching principle or the prudence convention do not have an obvious 'desirability characterisation'. The question 'Why?' is a natural one to ask of such conventions. That one does not stop theorising with general rules or conventions is also clear even if one views the reasoning from such conventions to standard setting decisions as nondeductive. If judgement is to be exercised in such decision-making surely there must be some considerations, one might call them 'principles' in some other sense than general rules, that guide such judgements. Faced with a clash between conventions it makes sense to ask what considerations are relevant to making the kinds of decisions or choices involved in the exercise of judgement in such reasoning. Another kind of reasoning may be involved in decision-making of this kind. Considering such a question might naturally lead to considering what is wanted from financial reporting, and this, in turn, may lead to identifying the kinds of objectives and qualitative characteristics expressed in conceptual frameworks.

The fixation with deductive reasoning appears to have resulted in the abandonment of the path of theorising that develops via conventions. In the original IASB conceptual framework and in the revised IASB/FASB conceptual framework, matching is referred to only once in connection with the recognition of expenses. It is clear that this 'income statement' approach must not conflict with the recognition of assets and liabilities given the 'balance sheet' approach which must come first. The priority of the 'balance sheet' approach draws attention away from the traditional conventions of matching and prudence which are more relevant to an 'income statement' approach. Prudence in the original IASB conceptual framework was a characteristic of reliability and apparently relates to both these approaches in that it affects both the balance sheet elements and the income statement elements. It is explained as 'the inclusion of a degree of caution in the exercise of the judgements needed in making the estimates required under conditions of uncertainty, such that assets or income are not overstated and liabilities or expenses are not understated' (IASB, 1989, §38). As noted earlier, prudence does not appear in the new framework. The *Basis for Conclusions* explains this is because it conflicts with neutrality (IASB, 2010, §BC3.27). Hans Hoogervorst explains that 'prudence was the inclusion of a degree of caution in the exercise of the judgements needed in making the estimates under conditions of uncertainty, such that assets or income are not overstated and liabilities or expenses are not understated' (Hoogervorst, 2012, p. 2). He goes on to say that prudence 'is still very much engrained in our standards' and goes on to give examples of this in IASB standards (Hoogervorst, 2012, p. 4). Although prudence is explained as a characteristic of judgements made by accountants in the context of making estimates under conditions of uncertainty the general rule of prudence is used by standard setters in developing standards. The point is that the rules in standards determine how accountants exercise such judgements. It is unclear whether there is still a residual, rather ghostly, convention of prudence that plays a part in standard setting. If so then this raises the question of the nature of the general rule expressed in the convention, whether it is a 'rule of thumb' or a rule on the 'practice' conception, and how it is involved in the derivation of specific rules from this convention.

The importance of general rules or conventions appears evident in other parts of the conceptual framework. After all, what are the recognition principle or the measurement principles but general rules to be used in deriving specific accounting standards? The recognition principle in the existing IASB conceptual framework states that 'an item that meets the definition of an element should be recognised if:

(a) it is probable that any future economic benefit associated with the item will flow to or from the entity; and
(b) the item has a cost or value that can be measured with reliability' (IASB, 2010, 4.38).

This could easily be expressed as a general rule, namely 'recognise items that meet the definition of an element if . . .' Similarly, the ideal measurement principle might be one that expresses a general rule 'recognise assets at . . .' where '. . .' is a measurement base. The problem with the existing framework is that such a rule is absent; instead, a number of measurement bases are allowed, and it is left to entities to choose the appropriate one. If there is a general measurement rule it is of the kind 'either measure the elements of financial statement at historical cost or current cost or realizable value or present value'. What is clear from a general rule of this kind is that decisions need to be made as to which of the alternatives is to be chosen. Again, some kind of reasoning is involved in making this kind of decision or choice, which is not deductive. This is why the choice of a measurement base is just that, a choice, and involves a decision which constitutes an exercise of judgement. This is why the FASB and IASB say that measurement is an 'underdeveloped area' of the conceptual framework and will be considered further in the revision of the framework (FASB/IASB, 2005, p. 12). Is this because the existing framework does not provide an adequate general rule? Does this mean the ideal framework would provide a rule or convention which eliminated the need for reasoning to a decision of this kind? What kind of rule or convention would replace it? One that enables the deduction of the measurement base to be applied to all these elements or that expresses some kind of 'rule of thumb' that would require the exercise of judgement to apply it?

It is an open question whether or not the conventions or general rules of accounting still are alive and kicking. If they still live, are they different than the traditional ones such as matching and prudence? The latter question raises the issue of whether or not standard setters need general rules or conventions to stand between some other kinds of 'principles' used in making standard setting decisions and the specific rules in standards. Further examination of this question will not be undertaken here. Instead the chapter will go on to consider the nature of the underlying 'principles' that either underpin standard setting decisions directly or provide the reasons for adopting conventions or general rules.

ANOTHER KIND OF 'PRINCIPLE'

Young suggests that what characterizes the conceptual framework approach is a move away from the traditional conception of theory as something setting out the conventions of accounting to something that arises out of the decision-usefulness approach to theorising. A principle of this kind would be something used in a 'logic of consequences' rather than a 'logic of appropriateness' involving rules that underpins the conventions approach. The decision to accept specific accounting rules is not conceived as a matter of reasoning from general rules to more specific ones but rather reasoning from certain ends or objectives to the desire to adopt specific rules that will meet these ends. Given that setting standards is an intentional action, the reasoning towards the desire to set standards is the kind of practical reasoning to intentional actions that has already been described.

The change in the direction of theorising about accounting throws ambiguity in the conception of a 'theory' of accounting. The AAA recognised this problem in understanding the nature of theories in their *Statement on Accounting Theory and Theory Acceptance* where it was recognised that there is no universally accepted 'theory' of accounting (AAA, 1977, p. 1). They recognised that there are different conceptions of theory in accounting which depend upon the purpose of the theorising. The explanations of the idea of a theory of accounting are not very helpful either. In one of the first books on accounting theory, published in 1922, written by Paton and called *Accounting Theory*, a theory of this kind was characterized as 'that body of doctrines, principles, important generalizations, which underlie the technical double-entry system, the valuation of assets attaching to the particular enterprise, and all phases of the art of accountancy'. It is contrasted with the rules of accounting that it 'underlies' and is characterized as a 'science' (Paton, 1922, p. 6). This distinction was made by a later writer who also distinguishes 'systems of rules relating to the practice of accounting and a theory of accounting' that sets out 'a more fundamental proposition or set of propositions' (Chambers, 1955, p. 17). It is not clear in what sense one proposition is more 'fundamental' than another. Baxter also explained 'theory' as 'the attempt to explain, in terms of fundamentals, what accounting is and what it tries to do' (Baxter, 1953, p. 415). The nature of such 'propositions' or 'fundamentals' and the kind of 'doctrines', 'principles' and 'generalisations' is not itself clear, nor is the sense in which such a theory 'underlies' the rules of accounting. Instead of characterising 'theories' in this way it might be more useful to refer to these activities in a more neutral manner. Theorising about accounting might be understood as the outcome of 'intellectual enquiry' or a 'process of exploring the rational foundations of accounting practice to suggest where and how improvements and developments may be made' (Macve, 1983, p.4). This characterization provides a good explanation of accounting theory in general in so far as it can be seen as involving some sort of 'thinking' about accounting. However, the kind of 'thinking' needs to be explained if this explanation is to be understood.

The change of direction in theorising about accounting was influenced by the 'science of decision' that followed the Second World War (Young, 2006, p. 584). This provided a stimulus to new ways of thinking about accounting with its emphasis on decision models, statistics and probability. It resulted in the 'formation of an economic-financial calculus approach' to decision-making and the 'connection of financial accounting to economic decision-making'. Decision-making was 'typically framed as a rational choice problem and conceptualized as an intentional, consequential, optimizing activity' where 'the decision maker specified the goals that would define an optimal solution, considered all alternatives and finally selected the alternative that maximized the likelihood of achieving the desired goal'. The idea emerged that this kind of decision-making required 'clear goals, and that improving the clarity of goals unambiguously improves the quality of decision-making' (Young, 2006, p. 585). Financial accounting decision-making was charged with the crime of making decisions without first considering what the goals were (Young, 2006, p. 586). It was in this context that A Statement of Basic Accounting Theory (ASOBAT) emerged with the emphasis on thinking about the goals of financial reporting.

One way of reading the change that was brought about by the decision-usefulness approach is to think of it as a move towards theorising about the action of standard setting that starts with what a standard setter wants to achieve by performing the intentional action of setting standards and then considers beliefs about what rules will achieve these ends. The conclusion is a desire to promulgate a rule. The kind of reasoning they undertake is practical reasoning of this kind:

> I (institutions/the legislature) want accounting/accountants to achieve objectives Y.
> I believe that promulgating rule X will achieve these objectives.
> I want to promulgate rule X.
>
> (adapted from Dennis, 2010b, p. 140)

What standard setters want can be characterized in various ways. In the first premise the desire is characterized as a desire to achieve an objective, but this could also be characterized as a desire to achieve a certain end as it is in the kind of 'means-end'/'instrumental'/practical reasoning described earlier. The second premise in the reasoning is rather condensed. Standard setters believe that by promulgating a rule the objectives will be achieved because they believe accountants will follow the rule because standard setters have promulgated the rule in an accounting standard, which will result in the fulfilment of the objectives. That accountants will follow the rules in accounting standards or the law will be assumed and will not be further examined. Together these premises are reasons for the action of promulgating standards. If rules in standards are promulgated for these reasons then the reasons give an explanation of the action undertaken. With a 'logic of appropriateness' the reasons that explain actions involve the mention of rules. With the decision-usefulness approach the reasons do not involve other rules but rather desires or objectives to be achieved by promulgating a rule.

The change in the direction of theorising is a change from a 'logic of appropriateness' to a 'logic of consequences'. With it came a change in the conception of 'principles' of accounting that are used in such reasoning from something that expresses a general rule to something that expresses what is wanted from accounting. In both senses 'principles' provide the standard setter with *reasons for promulgating accounting standards*. However, the kinds of reasons and the nature of the reasoning may be different. The conceptual framework exemplifies the change in theorising that came with the decision-usefulness approach. The conceptual framework is sometimes characterized as a 'theory' of financial reporting, and 'a perceived need for some kind of theoretical basis or 'conceptual framework' for financial reporting' has been felt in English-speaking countries for some decades' (Archer, 1993, p. 62). The kind of theory that emerged is one that expresses the desires that standard setters want to achieve in promulgating rules. Such desires are used in practical reasoning and are expressed in the kind of first premise set out in the reasoning expressed earlier. This reasoning includes further premises that express beliefs about which rules will fulfil these desires. The conclusion of such reasoning is a desire to promulgate rules of accounting.

The conceptual framework is meant to be a 'foundation' that is used in setting standards in the sense that it expresses that part of the reason for actions of standard setting that sets out the objectives or ends or desires the standard setter wants to achieve by accountants following those rules. The objectives expressed in the first premise form part of the 'foundation'/'frame of reference'/'framework' for standard setting. The 'principles' in a conceptual framework include expressions of desires—that is, the objective or purpose of promulgating standards. They may be called, as they are so called in the conceptual framework, a *statement of the objectives of financial reporting*. An example of such a desire is provided in the IASB conceptual framework, which states that 'the objective of general purpose financial reporting is to provide financial information about the reporting entity that is useful to existing and potential investors, lenders, and other creditors in making decisions about providing resources to the entity' (IASB, 2010, §OB2). This could be re-expressed as the expression of a desire in the following form:

> I want to promulgate rules that, if followed, will provide financial information about the reporting entity that is useful to existing and potential investors, lenders, and other creditors in making decisions about providing resources to the entity.

The 'I' in the statement is meant to be the standard setter, the user of the conceptual framework, who accepts the objectives statement and wants to promulgate a particular accounting standard that is believed will fulfil this objective if followed. This belief is an empirical statement to the effect that promulgating a particular accounting standard will result, causally, in the objectives of financial reporting being achieved. The conclusion of the reasoning expresses a desire to promulgate that standard: that is, 'I want to promulgate [a particular accounting standard]'. This insight needs to be explored further by looking more closely at the premises and at the reasoning that is used to make standard setting decisions. The desires expressed in a conceptual framework and how they are used to make standard setting decisions needs to be further considered.

THE DESIRES IN THE CONCEPTUAL FRAMEWORK

In a 'logic of consequences' where a standard setter is deciding what rules to promulgate, it was suggested in the previous chapter that the desire and the belief have to have *generality* given the generality inherent in a rule. The formulation of a desire that might be used to derive rules was suggested earlier—that is, 'I want to promulgate rules that, if followed, will provide financial information about the reporting entity that is useful to existing and potential investors, lenders and other creditors in making decisions about providing resources to the entity'. Given this desire the standard setter must look around to identify a rule that, if followed, will achieve the desired end. This is a factual matter which would be expressed by a belief that a certain rule would achieve this end. If the standard setter has such a desire and a belief, he may conclude that he wants to promulgate this rule.

The problem with the formulation of the desire premise is that it is not clear where the generality is located. It cannot be 'I always want to promulgate rules . . .', for this suggests that a standard setter must be always be wanting to promulgate rules. A premise of this kind is clearly 'insane' as a premise in practical reasoning (Anscombe, 1957, §33). Even the most ardent standard setter cannot be thought to be forever promulgating rules! This can be easily rectified by re-expressing the premise as '(Whenever I want to promulgate rules) I always want . . .'

Another problem arises with what to put in the '. . .' in the aforementioned sentence. Does the standard setter want to promulgate *some* rule that meets the desired end or perhaps *any* or *every* rule that does so? This might be called the problem of the *quantifier* that is included in the desire premise—that is, whether it is 'some' or 'any' or 'every'. If it is true that a standard setter wants *any* or *every* rule that meets a certain end or objective then standard setting is simplified. All the standard setter has to do is to identify a rule that will meet this end, and then they can conclude that they want to promulgate it. There is no *decision* or *choice* to be made. The reasoning is *deductive*, and conclusions follow from the premises necessarily. If the standard setter always wants to promulgate any or every rule that achieves the end in question, and if there is a particular rule that will achieve it, then the standard setter *must* want to promulgate it. If this is how the desire premise is to be formulated, what happens if there is more than one rule that would achieve the end in question? Say there were three rules that would achieve this end, rule X, rule Y and rule Z. This would mean the standard setter would have to conclude that she wants to promulgate rule X, rule Y and rule Z. If promulgating one rule that has the desired effect is incompatible with promulgating another that also has the desired end then *incompatible* conclusions would be drawn. At least one of the premises must be given up. If it is actually the case that both rule X and rule Y will always achieve an objective and rule X and rule Y are incompatible then the first premise—that is, the desire to promulgate *any* standard with the desired effect—appears suspect.

An alternative formulation of the premise '(Whenever I want to promulgate rules) I always want . . .' where '. . .' is replaced by 'some' will not solve the problem of what to do when more than one rule will meet the desired end. As long as the rule will meet the end then it could be a candidate for promulgation. So, if *either* rule X *or* rule Y *or* rule Z will meet the end then there is some rule that meets this end. Any of these rules could be wanted. The conclusion is a desire to promulgate either of these rules, but there is, as yet, no basis on which to choose between them. If the standard setter chooses one rather than the other then this choice is not *necessitated* by the premises.

In other words, the standard setter cannot deduce which to want to promulgate. There are two 'solutions' to this problem. The first solution modifies the rule that is to be promulgated. The desire to promulgate a rule could allow those who follow it to choose between *alternative* actions—that is, the rule is of the form 'Do either *A* or *B* or *C, etc.*' The standard setter allows the rule-follower to exercise *judgement* in deciding which of the alternatives to undertake. There is no basis provided in the rule to guide the rule-follower as to what to do. If it is left to the rule-follower to make the decision then he will have to bring in some other desires to help him adjudicate between the alternatives. The desires that prompt the standard setter to promulgate a rule do not justify any *one* of the alternatives.

If one of the alternatives is chosen by the standard setter then the reasoning involved is *not deductive*. There is no necessity, given the premises, in choosing one or the other of the rules. If the standard setter rules out one or other of the rules—that is, the standard setter exercises personal judgement in deciding between alternative rules—then there is some *other* desire that she brings to bear in choosing between them. What she has done, in effect, is to modify the desire itself so that *only one* of the rules actually meets the objective/end/desire in the first premise, which rules out all the other possible candidates. If this happens then only one rule will be deduced from the desire. The problem with this is in identifying what is wanted so there is always only one rule that fulfils the desire.

Both solutions have been adopted in setting standards in the past. In the U.S. the Committee on Accounting Procedure (CAP) was set up in 1938 to consider particular accounting problems and to recommend 'one or more alternative procedures as being definitely superior in its opinion to other procedures' (quoted in Zeff, 1972, p. 137). At their first meeting they rejected the approach that would have considered the 'principles' that were to be followed in deciding on recommendations of procedures to be adopted—that is, to spend time in formulating a 'theory' that would underpin such decisions. In effect, their solution was to allow alternatives rather than to re-formulate what was wanted from the rules recommended to exclude the necessity for alternatives. This approach was questioned in the 1950s and resulted in the attempt to formulate the 'principles' on which standard setting was to be founded, which culminated in the Moonitz and Sprouse publication (Moonitz and Sprouse, 1962) setting out accounting 'principles' in the early 1960s. The quest for 'principles' fizzled out in the face of criticism from the Accounting Principles Board and did not reemerge until the 1970s with the onset of the conceptual framework project undertaken by the FASB. In the UK, Stamp identified one of the essential components of a conceptual framework as the 'identification of a set of (ideally, mutually exclusive and collectively exhaustive) criteria to be used in choosing between alternative solutions to standard-setting problems' (Tweedie, 1993, p. xiv). In other words, the 'principles' in a conceptual framework should eliminate the need for standards to include alternatives. This conception appears to lie behind the idea of a 'principles-based' approach as one based on a conceptual framework where the need for alternatives in accounting standards is reduced if not eliminated. The conceptual framework is meant to provide 'the basic reasoning on which to consider the merits of alternatives' and 'narrows the range of alternatives to be considered' (FASB, 2001, 'Understanding the Issues'). In revising the conceptual framework the solution to the problem of alternatives is to change the 'principles' in the framework upon which standard setting decisions are made. This may not completely solve the problem if this only 'narrows' rather than eliminates the problem.

If deduction is used in reasoning from statements in a conceptual framework to the desire to promulgate rules in standards then the desire premise used in a 'logic of consequences' would be something like '(Whenever I want to promulgate rules) I always want to promulgate any/every rule that always meets end A'. Another problem arises where such a premise is used deductively to set standards. What happens if the standard setter identifies a rule but this rule will not meet the desired end on all occasions? This creates a problem if the rule is conceived on the 'practice' conception. This means the rule is to be followed on all occasions. If there is one occasion where following the rule does not meet the desired end then it is not true that that the standard setter always wants to promulgate a rule that meets end A, for the rule in question will not always meet this end. One way to overcome this problem is to specify that only rules which always meet this end are to be promulgated. This involves a modification of the desire premise to '(Whenever I want to promulgate rules) I always want to promulgate any/every rule that always meets end A'. If a conceptual framework is to be used deductively in deriving a desire to promulgate a standard then it has to conform to this kind of premise.

It is interesting to note that a premise like this could be re-expressed as '(Whenever I want to promulgate rules), always promulgate any/every rule that always meets end A'. Expressed in this way the desire premise looks like a general prescription to do something, namely to promulgate a rule in a standard which always meets a certain end. In the generic sense of a rule as 'a general prescription guiding conduct or action' (Twining and Miers, 1976, p. 48) it is possible to understand the desire premise as a rule that is given by standard setters to themselves that prescribes a course of action in general. Rules, in this generic sense, include 'precepts, regulations, rules of thumb, conventions, principles, guiding standards and even maxims' (Twining and Miers, 1976, p. 49). It thus makes sense to say that what is established in a conceptual framework is a 'principle' but that it is possible to understand a conceptual framework as setting out rules or what is wanted in setting rules. Statements of principles in a conceptual framework can be understood in either of these senses.

Wittgenstein remarked that the 'surface grammar' of a sentence sometimes conceals its 'depth grammar' (Wittgenstein, 1953, §664). This may be the case with 'general prescriptions' of this kind. They look like rules but actually behave like the expression of a desire. The difference between rules that really express desires and rules per se is that with the former the rule includes a quantifier that needs a value before the rule can be made operative. If a standard setter gives himself a prescription like '(Whenever I want to promulgate rules), always promulgate any/every rule that always meets end A', it is not clear what rules need to be promulgated until the quantifier 'any/every' is given a value. A 'principle', in this sense, would be a *rule with a hole*. To give it a value standard setters have to look around at actual rules and identify *any* or *every* one of them that meets an end A. Prescriptions of this kind cannot be followed without identifying the rules that constitute the values of the variable. This is similar to saying that if standard setters want to promulgate rules that achieve a certain end they have to identify what rules will achieve this end. They use such a desire in reasoning that also requires a belief about what rules will achieve this end. It is the same with the expression of the desire as a general prescription. It is not possible for the standard setter to know what to do to follow this prescription without being able to identify 'any' or 'every' rule that meets the end. The point is that although the desire can be expressed as a prescription it acts like the expression of a desire. Although its 'surface grammar' may be that of a prescription its 'depth grammar' is that of an expression of a desire. It is used in reasoning to a desire to promulgate a specific rule and requires another premise that expresses a belief that a specific rule will achieve the desire in question.

There is an important parallel between the kind of reasoning that occurs in standard setting and that which occurs in moral reasoning. There is a school of thought that says that moral reasoning requires the identification of the kind of universal principles that some standard setters assume are required in reasoning to the desire to promulgate accounting standards. This will now be briefly explored.

UNIVERSALISM IN MORAL REASONING

A Kantian system of morality identifies 'moral principles' that are used in deductive reasoning to a desire to perform actions that accord with such principles. Even here there is an ambiguity in the idea of a 'principle'. Is it a general rule that can be used to derive more specific rules that, if followed, result in specific actions that accord with the principles, or is it some kind of general desire that is to be fulfilled by specific actions? 'Principles' have two qualities. They are used in moral reasoning and are *universal*. As Kant puts it, you need to 'act as if the maxim of your action were to become through your will a universal law of nature' (Paton, 1948, pp. 29 and 30). The other quality is that 'principles' have *necessity*. Kant says that 'only *law* carries with it the concept of an *unconditioned*, and yet objective and so universally valid, *necessity*' (Kant, 1785, p. 80). Such 'principles' are called by Kant 'categorical imperatives'. Both these qualities might be expressed by 'principles' conceived as desires or as general rules. One way of understanding 'principles' as desires is to take them as an expression of *universal desires*. This would give to such 'principles' the form 'Always want to do [or perhaps, more realistically, (whenever you are considering what you ought to do) always want to do] anything/everything that will always result in X'. When one is considering what to do one considers beliefs about what actions will bring about X and then one draws a conclusion given that one wants to do anything/everything that will bring about the end.

A major problem with a moral system of this kind is that 'few moral judges are equipped with an exhaustive set or exceptionless moral principles by reference to which all their moral judgments are made' (Craig, 2005, p. 694). This kind of approach 'confronts a dilemma' that 'either our set of principles would be small and readily comprehensible . . . but would need to be framed in such general terms as to make their application to even the simplest cases a difficult matter to determine; or they would be framed in terms specific enough to make the assessment of their application to particular circumstances straightforward, but would thereby need to be so numerous and highly qualified as to be unusable' (Craig, 2005, p. 694). This is really the problem of formulating a universal desire in such a way that it allows a clear deduction of desires to act in particular circumstances that are acceptable to the person accepting such a principle.

The overall problem is that deduction is non-ampliative, in the sense that the conclusion is contained in the premises. If someone wants something universally—that is, wants the kind of thing set out in a universal premise of the kind indicated earlier—then they want anything that can be deduced from this premise. If they do not like the consequences—that is, the desire that is deduced—then they do not like the universal premise. Accepting the premise is accepting any consequences that can be deduced from it. This raises an important question about such premises—namely, how do you know that you always want something until you see what consequences follow from such a universal desire? One consequence may be that inconsistent rules are desired. Another problem is that it may reveal a desire to do something you do not actually want to do because you want something else more.

Another moral philosopher suggests a solution to this problem that preserves the universality of the 'principle' and its deductive use. The solution is to recognise that 'principles' are always capable of being reformulated in the light of the conclusions about what action is wanted that are deduced from the 'principle'. It is suggested that 'we are always setting precedents for ourselves . . . decision and principles interact throughout the whole field . . . suppose that we have a principle to act in a certain way in certain circumstances. Suppose then that we find ourselves in certain circumstances which fall under the principle, but which have certain other peculiar features, not met before, which make us ask "Is the principle really intended to cover cases like this, or is it incompletely specified—is there here a case belonging to a class which should be treated as exceptions?" Our answer to this question will be a decision, but a decision of principle . . . If we decide that this should be an exception, we thereby modify the principle by laying down an exception to it' (Hare, 1952, p. 65). If we decide that we do not actually want what is supposed to be universally desired because the consequences that may be deduced from it are not acceptable then we change the 'principle'. Moral reasoning is deductive and involves universal premises—that is, 'universal prescriptions'—but they need to be continually revised in the light of the deductions that can be made from them.

Rawls suggests an escape from a situation where 'principles' have to be continuously revised. He suggests the method of 'reflective equilibrium' whereby one begins by identifying one's moral judgements, or what might be called 'intuitions' or an 'original position', and then tries to construct 'principles' that provide the best fit with these judgements. The judgements or intuitions themselves may be modified until they reach some kind of 'equilibrium' or 'reflective equilibrium' or moral 'principles' (Scanlon, T., in Craig, 2005, p. 696). The result is rather similar to that suggested by Hare. One arrives at universal 'principles' from which one can deduce moral actions one can accept. Rawls thinks that some 'equilibrium' in this process can be reached whereas Hare would seem to think of this as only provisional and the 'principles' as subject to continual revision. This idea has found favour in the accounting literature in understanding the role of the conceptual framework. Power suggests that 'the function of a conceptual framework for financial accounting is loosely analogous to Rawls' "original position" in the sense of articulating an underlying "constructivist" approach to accounting policy'. He goes on to say that 'a conceptual framework is not an ultimate foundation in any classical sense but a point of reference in the network of accounting standards and practices that serves to "organize" thinking about them' (Power, 1993, p. 53). In other words, the conceptual framework is the result of a 'reflective equilibrium'. In the same way it might be asked whether the conceptual framework is some kind of 'finalised' equilibrium or is like Hare's 'principles', only provisional and subject to revision.

What is common to all these approaches to moral decision-making is that they share an adherence to the idea that it is possible to identify what is desired in moral actions so that they can be used in means-end or practical reasoning of the deductive kind. This approach is implicit in the 'rational comprehensive' or 'root' approach or a 'hard systems' methodology that Archer draws attention to in the accounting literature (Archer, 1993, p. 81). A 'hard systems' approach is one where 'problems can be expressed as the search for an efficient means of reaching a defined objective or goal; once goals or objectives are defined, then systematic appraisal of alternatives, helped by various techniques, enables the problem (now one of selection) to be solved' (Checkland 1981, quoted in Archer, 1993, p. 81). The 'root' method is one where objectives are identified in advance of the use of empirical analysis to identify the means to achieving this end (Archer, 1993, p. 82). These approaches characterize the underlying approach that appears to lie behind the attempt to construct a conceptual framework or 'theory' of accounting. Archer suggests that alternative methods or methodologies could have been considered by the FASB in constructing a conceptual framework but were ignored. These include 'soft systems' methodologies and a 'hybrid' approach that combines the merits of the best of the 'root' method with the 'branch' method in a 'gross balance method' developed by Rowe (Archer, 1993).

There is no space to consider the merits of these alternative methodologies. What appears questionable in the 'root' approach and in the systems of moral decision-making is the assumption that what is required in such approaches or systems are 'principles' that are to be used in *deducing* desires for actions either of the moral kind or actions such as promulgate accounting standards in a standard setting situation. The underlying assumption is that practical reasoning or means-end reasoning is deductive and, hence, needs the kind of premises that enable deductive reasoning to be used in deriving desires to act. The influence of this idea on the development of the conceptual framework is very important. This will now be explored.

A NONDEDUCTIVE VIEW OF PRACTICAL REASONING USING THE CONCEPTUAL FRAMEWORK

In the quotations set out earlier, a number of writers have commented upon the deductive ideal assumed when the conceptual framework is used to derive accounting standards. As noted previously, Power identifies an assumption that if deductive reasoning is not used in decision-making of this kind then the result is, in some way, defective. At least one former standard setter doubts whether the conceptual framework is actually used in this way. Lennard argues that 'the Framework does not (and probably should not) provide axioms from which specific accounting requirements can be deduced with ineluctable logic . . . [it indicates] a direction of travel . . . The accounting standards that will result from the . . . Framework cannot be deduced from its first two chapters' (Lennard, 2007, p. 53). Others may agree. An ad hominem argument to those standard setters who do believe it is used deductively would be to ask them exactly how a conceptual framework is used in practice to deduce standards. If a conceptual framework is not to be used to deduce standards the question arises as to what kind of reasoning is to be used in deriving the desire to promulgate standards from the premises provided by the conceptual framework. How can such reasoning be used to indicate a 'direction of travel'?

The fact that some other kind of reasoning to an intentional action might be used to derive a desire to act has already been illustrated when actors reason to intentional actions on specific occasions. It was suggested that practical reasoning of this kind is not generally deductive. The reasoning started with the expression of a desire to achieve some end and included a belief that performing an action would fulfil the desire, and the conclusion of a desire to perform the action was derived nondeductively. Where the action is an action of adopting a rule then it was suggested that the premises have to be modified to include generalities. For example, because the acceptance of a rule is accepting something to be followed on a number of occasions, what is wanted must be wanted generally—that is, on the occasions where the rule is to be followed. Similarly, the belief is not a belief that on only one occasion performing an action will achieve the desired end, but where a rule is involved the belief has a generality in so far as one has to believe that, in general, at least on the numerous occasions when the rule is to be followed, acting in accord with the rule will fulfil the desired end. Although the premises have to have the requisite generality it does not follow that they have to have the kind of universality that would be required if the reasoning involved was deductive.

The universal premise required for deductive reasoning was expressed as '(Whenever I want to promulgate rules), always promulgate any/every rule that always meets end A'. There are three ways in which the universality of the desire premise involved in reasoning to the desire to follow or promulgate a rule can be modified to reflect a generality that falls short of universality. The first way would be to replace the phrase 'always promulgate a rule that meets end A' with 'always promulgate a rule that meets one, or several of, the ends X, Y or Z' or, alternatively, 'generally promulgate a rule that meets end X' and 'generally promulgate a rule that meets end Y' and 'generally promulgate a rule that meets end Z'. If a premise of this kind is to be used in reasoning to a rule then it is left to those who accept or promulgate rules to decide, using their judgement, which of the generally desired ends is to be met when a particular rule is accepted. In effect, the desire premise identifies a number of possible ends that are to be achieved by the acceptance of rules, and these have to be considered when the decision about what rule to accept is made. Although a desire of this kind may be supplemented with some guidance about the weighting of such desires there may be no way of weighting them so they can be used to express a universal desire that can be used in deductive reasoning. What desires are identified in the conceptual framework?

THE DESIRES IN THE CONCEPTUAL FRAMEWORK AGAIN

The alternative formulation of the desire premise where universal desires are replaced by ones that include generality that falls short of universality recognises it may be difficult to express a desire the standard setter *always wants*. What happens if she also wants some other end that is incompatible with it? If the reasoning is deductive then the addition of other premises will not undermine the conclusion. In other words, deduction is, as noted earlier, 'erosion-proof'. If the standard setter decides he does not want to promulgate a rule that meets the desired ends because some other desire takes priority then the original reasoning cannot be deductive, for the introduction of another premise, one that states a desire to achieve something else, undermines the previous conclusion. Clearly, if a standard setter 'always wants' to achieve some end and promulgating a rule will achieve it, and if they conclude they do not want to promulgate the rule because it will not achieve some other desire, then they do not always want the end that prompted the rule in the first place. The desires meant to underpin deductive reasoning must be those that are always wanted regardless of whatever else is wanted. There is no need to choose between desires—that is, there is no need to exercise judgement in making decisions about what is wanted.

It was suggested that the objectives statement in the conceptual framework could be re-expressed as 'I want to promulgate rules that, if followed, will provide financial information about the reporting entity that is useful to existing and potential investors, lenders and other creditors in making decisions about providing resources to the entity'. The evolution of the objectives statement was rather a tortured process. Although the decision-usefulness approach was agreed, one of the issues that needed to be resolved in the IASB/FASB project to revise the conceptual framework was the need to decide on which external decisions and which decision-makers were to be the primary focus in the objectives statement (FASB/IASB, 2005, p. 4). In other words, conceptual frameworkers had to decide which of the 'wide range of decision makers' they wanted to provide useful information for in financial reporting and for what purposes they wanted to provide information. Deciding on this would determine what accounting standards would be promulgated to meet these needs.

There are a number of problems in deciding on these matters which surfaced in the 'due process' which led to the adoption of the new chapters 1 and 3 of the framework. The first problem that was dealt with was whether there was a need to specify a group of primary users whose needs standard setters should want to meet. The argument the board accepted was that without specifying primary users the conceptual framework 'would risk becoming unduly abstract or vague' (IASB, 2010, BC1.14). The reasons given for the selection of primary users were that such users 'have the most critical and immediate need for the information in financial reports and many cannot require the entity to provide the information to them directly'. Moreover, it was acknowledged that both the IASB and the FASB has responsibilities to focus on the needs of such users as 'participants in capital markets'. A further argument was made that meeting the needs of such users should also meet the needs of other users (IASB, 2010, BC1.16). The second problem that arises from the discussion paper that was issued by the IASB/FASB was the fact that it focused on the use of information for resource allocation decisions, which prompted a debate about whether or not there should be a separate stewardship objective in the framework. The IASB/FASB acknowledged that users make resource allocation decisions as well as stewardship decisions about whether management has made efficient and effective use of the resources provided. By a series of manoeuvres the desire to provide information to the primary users in making decisions about providing resources to the entity became the desire to provide information about the resources of the entity, claims against the entity and how efficiently and effectively the entity's management and governing board have discharged their responsibilities to use the entity's resources which also assist stewardship decisions. It was argued by the board that 'in most cases, information designed for resource allocation decisions would also be useful for assessing management's performance' (IASB, 2010, BC1.26).

It is interesting to reflect on why a desire to meet the needs of a certain kind of user and a desire for the identification of one thing such users need were important in the conceptual framework. If standard setters agree that they always want financial statements to provide one kind of information for one kind of user then this might be able to be used in deductive reasoning to rules for providing financial information in financial statements. Given this universal desire the standard setter has only to identify a rule that will fulfil this desire in order to deduce that she wants to promulgate a rule that results in this information being provided. If information is to be used by a number of users who want different things then the requirement to provide certain kinds of information in the conceptual framework to meet user needs may involve weighing the different needs and deciding which are to be met by promulgating a particular rule of accounting expressed in an accounting standard. The reasoning involved will not be deductive and, hence, some *judgement* may be required in drawing conclusions about what rules to promulgate.

It is instructive to follow the thought processes by which this universal desire is agreed upon. Given the desire in the objectives statement to provide information useful in making decisions about providing resources to the entity it is stated that these decisions involve buying, selling or holding equity and debt instruments and providing or settling loans and other forms of credit. These decisions depend upon the returns that are expected from an investment in those instruments, and these expectations depend on the assessment of the amount, timing and uncertainty of (the prospects for) future net cash inflows to the entity. To make the assessment of future cash inflows there is a need for information about the resources of the entity, claims against the entity and how efficiently and effectively the entity's management and governing board have discharged their responsibilities to use the entity's resources. This information is also useful for decisions by existing investors, lenders and other creditors who have the right to vote on or otherwise influence management's actions—in other words, in making stewardship decisions, though the term 'stewardship' is not used (IASB, 2010, §§OB2–4). Given the need for such information, standard setters want to promulgate rules that result in the provision of such information.

What is happening in the conceptual framework is that the desire to provide information about the resources of the entity, claims against the entity and how efficiently and effectively the entity's management and governing board have discharged their responsibilities to use the entity's resources is derived from the desire to provide information useful in making decisions about providing resources to the entity. It is worth considering the logical nature of the statements that enable the derivation to take place. The statement regarding the nature of the decisions about providing resources to the entity appears to be a statement about the *meaning* of the phrase 'decisions about providing resources to the entity'. The nature of the statement that these decisions depend upon the returns expected is unclear. It appears like an *empirical* statement that says that, as a matter of fact, those who make such decisions base them on expected returns. The next transition again appears to rely upon a statement of the *meaning* of the expression 'expected returns'. This means 'future cash flows'. The next transition to the need for information about resources, etc. and the efficiency and effectiveness of management appears to be an *empirical* statement about how information about future cash flows is actually derived by those who use such information.

This mix of empirical statements and statements of meaning in the derivation of one desire from another is problematic. It may be thought that the necessity of the desire derived from another desire is based on a meaning connection that enables the one desire to be deduced from another. So, if someone wants A and, as a matter of meaning, that if A then B, then someone wants B. If someone wants information to make decisions about providing resources to an entity and this means decisions about buying, selling, etc. then they want information to make decisions about buying, selling, etc. If someone wants information about buying, selling, etc. and if wanting information about this is wanting information about cash flows then they want information about cash flows. However, if it is only an empirical matter that those who want information about buying, selling, etc. want information about cash flows then the derivation depends upon the truth of the empirical statement. Is it necessarily true that everyone who makes such a decision uses information of this kind? If only some, or even most, people make decisions in this way one cannot deduce that information of this kind *must* be needed. What evidence is there to support an empirical statement that decisions of this kind are necessarily made using information about future cash flows?

That some kind of meaning connection underlies the derivation of desires in the conceptual framework is implied, without explicitly stating it, by Young (2006). It is not that making a buying/selling, etc. decision necessarily involves using information about future net cash inflows but rather users *of a certain kind* necessarily make these decisions by using information about future net cash inflows. The reason they do this is that users in this sense—they could be designated 'users' to distinguish them from actual users—are *constructs*. Such 'users' act in accordance with how finance theory says they must act. Such 'users' make decisions about buying/selling, etc. using information about future net cash inflows. That 'users' make decisions in this way is implied by the *meaning of 'user'*. It follows deductively that if you want to provide information to 'users' then you will want to provide information about future net cash inflows. Young argues that although there is much emphasis on the information needs and decision processes of actual users of financial statements in the process of developing conceptual frameworks very little empirical knowledge has been obtained about their information needs and decision processes. Those who construct conceptual frameworks may not be interested in how *actual* investors make decisions but with what information *should be used* to make decisions. As she puts it, they are more interested in *constructing* 'the category of financial statement users' (Young, 2006, p. 580)—that is, the category of 'users'. The talk about constructing a category of users is really a matter of *constructing the meaning* of the word 'user'.

It is worth considering why conceptual frameworkers have a predilection for the constructed user against the actual user. Young (2006) explains this predilection in terms of political decisions desired to restrict the development of reporting requirements (Young, 2006, p. 597). This follows a line of thought expressed by Hines, who states that 'it is well understood and accepted today that the setting of accounting principles is a political process' (1989, p. 80). It is not the objective of this chapter to consider the political nature of standard setting. Its objective is to suggest that the predilection for constructing 'user' needs may be explained not by political processes but by the assumption that standard setting is a deductive process that proceeds from universal desires from which standards can be deduced. This is facilitated by the definition of 'users', which enables the desires that underpin standard setting to express universal desires. As Young puts it, 'these strategies distance the potentially messy readers of financial statement from the standard setting process' (Young, 2006, p. 591). The fact that there may be different users with different desires for information might mean the standard setter has to use judgement in determining which of the users and their needs are to be given priority. Choices or decisions would have to be made that are avoided if only one desire is identified that will always be used in reasoning to standard setting decisions. The adoption of a 'top down' approach to standard setting involving a conceptual framework has been called the 'first step' toward the reformation of accounting practice and has as its objective the desire to identify 'an authoritative set of deductive concepts' (Miller, 1990, p. 24). This deductive approach to constructing a theory of accounting has been described by Hendriksen (1977) as 'the process of starting with objectives and postulates and, from these, deriving logical principles that provide the bases for concrete or practical applications' (Hendriksen, 1977, p. 7). There are two steps in this approach. The first step is the assumption that rules of accounting can be deduced from the premises set out in a conceptual framework or accounting theory. The second step is to construct desires that can be used in such deductions. Wittgenstein once wrote, 'the first step is the one that altogether escapes notice' (Wittgenstein, 1953, §308). It is often the most important step. It is the assumption that gets overlooked.

The conceptual framework has attempted to convert practical reasoning into deductive reasoning by using various strategies. In order to deal with the problem that a standard setter may want to meet the needs of various users and that these needs may not coincide, the conceptual framework has not only determined which of the users are 'primary'—in other words, only to be considered—but has then defined 'user' in such a way that such users have defined needs in order to ensure the needs of 'users' do not conflict. These needs are then used to determine what is relevant financial information—that is, information that meets the needs of these 'users'. Although 'users' includes three different kinds of user the information they need is determined by the idea of 'users', and there is no conflict in what they want. There is no sense in which a standard can meet one user's needs more strongly than those of another. The conceptual framework goes on to say that financial information used by 'users' must have the quality of 'faithful representation', which is defined in terms of completeness, neutrality and freedom from error. The possibility that these qualities may pull in different directions is defused by the strategy that the maximization of these desires is desired rather than just the desire for these various qualities. This is evident from the statement in the conceptual framework about the characteristics of 'faithful representation'. It states that 'perfection is seldom, if ever, achievable. The Board's objective is to maximise those qualities to the extent possible' (IASB, 2010, QC12). There is thus no need for the standard setter to decide which of the desires is to be given the strongest weighting in order to make a decision. There is a necessity to choose the standard that maximizes these desires. The appearance that the conclusion follows without judgement is clearly undermined by the fact that determining what standard maximizes these desires is a matter of judgement. How this is done is not determined by any explanation of what 'maximises' actually means. Judgement is also required to determine what having these qualities actually means. It was suggested that the meaning of the expressions that denote these qualities is vague and that it is left to the judgement of the standard setter to determine their meaning in particular circumstances. The appearance that judgement is eliminated by the use of deductive reasoning is undermined by the fact that judgement creeps in 'by the back door'. A similar strategy is adopted by the inclusion of enhancing qualitative characteristics and the introduction of a cost constraint. The impression that these characteristics can be quantified and that the standard that maximizes these characteristics is to be reasoned deductively makes it look as though judgement in drawing a conclusion is eliminated. This appearance is undermined by the need to exercise such judgement in both determining which characteristics of a standard are more strongly enhancing and also in understanding what are, in reality, vague expressions. The impression that the 'principles' in the conceptual framework offer the standard setter the chance to deduce a conclusion in reasoning to a desire to promulgate a standard that obviates the need to exercise judgement is managed only by a fudge. Judgement is introduced elsewhere in order to achieve this end. What would an alternative conceptual framework look like, and what kind of reasoning would be used in making standard setting decisions?

AN ALTERNATIVE CONCEPTUAL FRAMEWORK

An alternative way of conceiving a conceptual framework is to take it as expressing *general* desires that are used in conjunction with beliefs to derive standards in accordance with *nondeductive* practical reasoning. The desires in the conceptual framework are not expressions of something *universally* wanted but rather expressions of something *generally* desired. The premise in the practical reasoning is not 'I always want *X*' but 'I generally want *X*'. Given this premise and the belief premise that a standard will fulfil the desire, the standard setter *may* conclude, but does not *have* to, that he wants to promulgate the standard. However, the conclusion is not *deduced* from the premises but rather derived by practical reasoning of a nondeductive kind. If you want to achieve an end and you believe a certain action will achieve it there is no necessity in concluding that you want to perform this action. If you add another premise, say another desire you wish to fulfil, and you believe the action in question will frustrate the fulfilment of this desire, then you may alter your conclusion and decide not to do it. In other words, the argument is not 'erosion-proof'. If you want to achieve several ends and the action in question will achieve all of them then you may want to perform the action more strongly than if only one or two of your desires will be met by the action. Some judgement is required in deciding whether, and how much, one wants to perform the action.

This is arguably the case in standard setting examples. The standard setter may want a number of different things in setting an accounting standard. She may want to meet the needs of various users of financial information. The problem is that different users may have different needs. If a standard meets more of these needs than another then the desire to promulgate this standard may be stronger. If a standard meets these needs but does so more comprehensively than others then the desire to promulgate this standard may be *stronger*. It may be that a standard meets the desires of more users than another and in a more comprehensive manner, but adding that it may be more costly than another and that the benefits do not outweigh the costs may result in another standard being chosen. The desire to promulgate the standard is not '*erosion-proof*' because the addition of new premises undermines the conclusion that this is wanted. The desire to promulgate a standard does not appear to follow necessarily from the premises, and some decision or judgement in drawing the conclusion appears to be necessary. In other words, the reasoning is *ampliative*. All these qualities suggest that the reasoning is not deductive. The reasoning starts not with a *universal* desire but with *general* desires that are to be met by the promulgating standards. An alternative way of viewing the identification of objectives and qualitative characteristics in the conceptual framework is that they set out general desires that are to be used in nondeductive practical reasoning in order to derive a desire to promulgate an accounting standard. This involves an inevitable exercise of judgement in determining whether the conclusion does follow from the premises. Indeed, that judgement is exercised in reasoning simply means the reasoning involved is not deductive. As such, there is no necessity in the conclusions drawn by such reasoning.

Skinner has suggested that accounting standards are a response to the inadequacy of accounting theory that would enable individuals 'to reach logical and practical conclusions to the issues that confront us in the real world'. He goes on to say that 'our present conceptual framework has failed to go that far'. As a response to this problem 'the profession has, over the years, developed standards reflecting collective judgments arrived at with due process' (Skinner, 1995/2005, p. 147). It is not clear why 'accounting theory' is inadequate. It may be that its inadequacy is thought to result from a failure to provide something that could be used to *deduce* accounting treatment in practical situations. This may appear to make any derivation *illogical*. Deriving conclusions using a 'theory' that does not allow for deductions about what to do in accounting situations could be described as involving an exercise of judgement in the sense explained by the CICA, referred to earlier. The fact that the reasoning is not deductive suggests a general characterisation of the process of exercising judgement as *a process of reasoning which is not deductive*. In the absence of a framework that could be used deductively it may be better that a standard setter should undertake this reasoning to avoid the problem of different people deriving different treatment from the 'theory'. It may be better for standard setters to exercise 'collective judgement' than accountants to exercise *individual* judgement.

This understanding of the nature of judgement accounts for another contention of the FASB/IASB that underpins their decision to undertake the new conceptual framework project. They argue that the conceptual framework itself should be agreed upon rather than 'personal'. If 'personal conceptual frameworks' are used in standard setting then agreement on standard setting issues may not be reached (FASB/IASB, 2005, p. 2). The assumption here is that if there is an agreed conceptual framework then individual standard setters will agree on accounting standards. This might be the case if the conceptual framework enabled deductive links between the statements in the conceptual framework and the conclusion about what standards to formulate. If the links are not deductive, though, then it might be possible for different members of the standard setting body to derive different conclusions from the conceptual framework. In other words, they may be able to exercise judgement in deciding what standards to promulgate because the process of reasoning is not deductive. The fact that judgement may be exercised in using a conceptual framework which states general, but not universal, desires does not mean that those exercising judgement can do *anything at all*. The whole point of including general desires in a conceptual framework is that these determine what is generally to be wanted, which provides a constraint on what standards can be desired. Although exercising judgement involves making decisions or choices, not *any* decisions or choices at all are allowed. The general desires in the conceptual framework provide constraint but are not a straightjacket.

One motive for the conception of the conceptual framework as something from which accounting standards can be deduced is that such a conceptual framework would eliminate the exercise of judgement from standard setting decisions. It is interesting to note that the predilection for 'rules-based' accounting standards also appears to be motivated by a desire to eliminate judgement in the application of accounting standards. This can also be understood as the attempt to establish rules whose application is deducible from the meaning of the expressions used in the standard and where no choices or decisions have to be made in following it. The alternative view of a conceptual framework as something that expresses only general and not universal desires suggests judgement is not eliminated from standard setting by the construction of a conceptual framework.

However, constructing an agreed framework that is used in collective decision-making by a standard setter who follows 'due process' may allow the inevitable judgements that have to be made in using such a framework to be agreed. In other words, it is not that a conceptual framework eliminates judgement. Judgement cannot be avoided where reasoning is not deductive even if there is an agreed framework for making decisions about accounting standards. However, agreement on judgements—'collective judgement', as it might be called—might be reached by collective nondeductive reasoning in the context of applying the conceptual framework to standard setting situations. This may be what is meant by the statement in the *Preface to IFRSs* that 'the conceptual framework also provides a basis for the use of judgement in resolving accounting issues' (IASB, 2010, §8).

SUMMARY

This chapter considers how accounting theories and conceptual frameworks are used by standard setters in making decisions about what standards to promulgate. Given that standard setting is an intentional action it is suggested there are two ways in which theories or frameworks can give reasons for standard setting decisions. The first way is by providing general rules that can be used to derive the more specific rules that appear in accounting standards. This approach uses a 'logic of appropriateness' where the reasons for standard setting decisions are made by reference to rules. This approach can be seen in the attempt to establish conventions of accounting. Understanding this approach is hampered by the assumption that the general rules are supposed to be followed on all occasions. The work of Rawls was used to show that there are two conceptions of rules. In the 'practice' conception, rules are conceived as those that are always to be followed. If such rules are accepted they can be used to deduce more specific rules. It was suggested that it is unlikely that such general rules can be established. A more realistic conception of rules is to conceive of them as 'rules of thumb' that are followed in general but may be overridden where following them will not always achieve the ends for which they are adopted. This means that such rules may be used to derive more specific rules but that there may be clashes with other generally accepted rules that need to be resolved through the use of judgement. This only means that such rules are not used to deduce other rules but to derive them using nondeductive reasoning.

Another approach to theorising was identified using a 'logic of consequences'. On this approach the ends or objectives of promulgating rules are identified—that is, what is wanted from such rules—and these are used in practical reasoning to a desire to promulgate standards by considering beliefs about what specific standards will result in the fulfilment of these desires. It was suggested that although the desires that are used in such reasoning have to have generality, given the generality of rules, they do not have to be universally desired—that is, desired on every occasion of standard setting. The idea that the desires should be universal is explored by looking at the analogy of moral reasoning. It was suggested that as with moral reasoning, the identification of universal desires is unlikely to be acceptable in the financial reporting context. The attempt to identify such desires in a conceptual framework accounts for the move to identify an 'ideal user' whose desires have the universality that can underpin universal desires in a conceptual framework. It was suggested that this kind of move is prompted by the desire to provide a framework that can be used to deduce standard setting decisions that will avoid the exercise of judgement by standard setters. It was argued that a more acceptable framework is one that identifies what is wanted in financial reporting in terms of general desires that are used in nondeductive practical reasoning that requires standard setters to exercise judgement in making standard setting decisions.

These two approaches to providing a theory or framework for standard setting decisions give rise to two concepts of 'principles'. 'Principles' can be conceived as general rules or as general desires. Given that standard setting decisions are meant to be based on 'principles' in a conceptual framework, standards that are 'principles-based' can be understood as either standards based on general rules or based on general desires.

4   Kinds of Rules in Accounting Standards

In the previous chapter it was suggested that where standard setters decide to promulgate accounting standards by considering what they want to achieve by this intentional action their decision is guided by a 'logic of consequences'. Conceptual frameworks were characterized as a kind of theory that expresses these objectives or desires. The idea that the 'principles' in such a framework express general desires that fall short of universality and that they are used in nondeductive reasoning to a desire to promulgate accounting standards was suggested. Given desires of this kind, the practical reasoning to decisions about what standards are to be promulgated proceeds by considering beliefs that specific standards will achieve what is wanted in promulgating standards.

This next stage is not necessarily undertaken by standard setters. They might prescribe to those who are to follow standards the objectives to be achieved by their actions. In other words, they might simply state in a standard, 'Do something that will bring it about that . . . ' where '. . .' are the objectives that are to be achieved—that is, the ends that are desired—by the action to be undertaken. It would then be left to those who follow the standards to consider beliefs about what specific actions will achieve these ends or objectives or to consider what rules might be established for them to follow that will achieve what is desired. The reasoning from the desires or objectives to actions is to be left to those who follow the standards and is not undertaken by standard setters. If judgement is exercised in such reasoning then this, again, is not undertaken by standard setters but is left to those who follow the standards.

This kind of approach might be dubbed, using a term adopted by the SEC, a 'principles-only' approach. The SEC describes standards developed with this approach as 'high-level standards with little if any operational guidance. A principles-only approach often provides insufficient guidance to make the standards reliably operational. As a consequence, principles-only standards typically require preparers and auditors to exercise judgment in accounting for transactions and events without providing a sufficient structure to frame that judgment' (SEC, 2003, p. 14). This would seem an accurate description of standards that said something like 'Do something that will bring it about that . . . ' This kind of approach is not further explored here. Instead it is assumed standard setters will go on to consider beliefs as to what rules will, if promulgated, achieve the objectives or ends in question.

One problem standard setters have to deal with is the problem of what happens when standards are not believed to achieve the desires expressed in a conceptual framework on all occasions to which they apply. It was suggested that where the intentional action is the acceptance of a rule then both the desire and the belief in practical reasoning to this action must have generality. This includes not only the generality of the desire, the fact that whatever is wanted must be wanted on the numerous occasions where following the rule is envisaged, but also the generality of the belief—that is, the belief that following the rule will meet the desires identified in general, on the numerous occasions where following the rule is envisaged. What happens, though, if the standard setter does not have such a belief? What does he do when he believes following a rule envisaged will not always achieve these objectives?

There are a number of ways of dealing with this problem that are explored in this chapter. The standard setter can simply accept that in promulgating such a rule there may be circumstances where the objectives will not be met. She may decide this is acceptable. If the objective is generally wanted but not universally desired then she may argue that as long as the rule, if followed, will achieve these desires *in general* even if *not always* then the rule is useful and should be promulgated. A problem only arises if the desires have to be achieved always—that is, if they have a universality—for then the failure to achieve them on all occasions undermines the claim that they are always wanted. If the standard setter always wants to achieve an end and promulgating a rule will not always achieve it then the standard setter must either give up wanting to promulgate the rule or give up the universal desire. This shows that certain combinations of conceptions are not possible. If desires are universal and rules must be followed on all occasions—that is, they are rules on the 'practice' conception—then either rules that will not fulfil the universal desires on all occasions are not promulgated or some way of dealing with those cases where they will not fulfil them must be found. If desires are universal and rules are conceived as 'rules of thumb' then if following the rule on an occasion will not fulfil the desire then it will be overridden. Judgement will have to be exercised by those following the standards to decide whether or not to override them. Another solution is to include exceptions in the rule so that the circumstances where following the rule will not achieve the universal desire are excluded from the ambit of the rule. That there are different conceptions of rules, as identified in the work of Rawls, was considered when we examined the idea that 'principles' might be conceived of as general rules that are used to derive more specific ones. It was suggested that general rules could be seen as 'rules of thumb' rather than rules on the 'practice' conception and that such general rules might allow the derivation of specific rules by nondeductive reasoning.

In this chapter the distinction between these two conceptions of rules is used to throw light on how standard setters might approach the problem of how to deal with rules that may not achieve the objectives of the rule on all occasions. This also throws light on the distinction between accounting standards that are 'principles-based' and those that are 'rules-based'. This distinction is often made using the idea of judgement or professional judgement. This is acknowledged as important in financial reporting (Institute of Chartered Accountants of Scotland; see ICAS, 2006). 'Rules-based' accounting standards are characterized as those that 'reduce or eliminate the exercise of professional judgement' (ICAS, 2006, p. 8) whereas 'principles-based' standards are those that require 'the use of judgement by preparers, auditors and regulators' (ICAS, 2006, p. 1; Schipper, 2003, p. 61). The use of judgement has already been referred to at several points in this book. The conceptual framework is meant to assist the judgement of standard setters in promulgating standards. Where the conceptual framework includes desires that are wanted generally but not universally, judgement must be exercised in deciding which of the desires is to be given priority on particular occasions where standards are being considered. Judgement may have to be exercised in deciding between measurement bases or conventions. It was suggested that the process of exercising judgement should be conceived as *a process of reasoning to decisions where the reasoning is not deductive.* This is evident in all the examples of exercising judgement considered so far. This insight will be explored a little further.

PROFESSIONAL JUDGEMENT

Much has been written lately on the importance of judgement, or professional judgement, in financial reporting. The *Final Report* of the Advisory Committee on Improvements to Financial Reporting (ACIFR) to the United States Securities and Exchange Commission (SEC) comments on the increased focus on judgement arising from changes in the regulation, the greater use of fair value and the focus on 'principles-based standards' (ACIFR, 2008, p. 88). Elsewhere the SEC has acknowledged it is impossible to eliminate professional judgment in the application of accounting standards (SEC, 2003, p. 16). The Institute of Chartered Accountants in Scotland have suggested that the balanced exercise of judgment is the key to true and fair financial reporting and that 'principles-based accounting standards' require the use of judgement (ICAS, 2006, p. 1). Schipper, a former member of the FASB, agrees with this and observes that International Financial Reporting Standards are meant to be standards of this kind (Schipper, 2003; Schipper, 2005). The chief executive officers of six large international accountancy firms suggest that a reform agenda should include a move towards such standards where the use of judgment should become the norm (Global Public Policy Symposium, 2008). Speaker after speaker at the 2006 AICPA National Conference commented that professional judgment is indispensable in auditing and financial reporting (Deloitte, 2006, p. 1). The importance for auditing is clear in International Auditing Standards, or ISAs (see IAASB, 2010, ISA 200, A23). Although there is general agreement on the important of judgement in financial reporting and auditing there are a number of different kinds of judgement that might be exercised (CICA, 1988).

The CICA definition of 'judgement' as 'the process of making a choice, a decision, leading to action' has already been given in the previous chapter. They then go on to explain what is required for judgement to be *professional*. The latter 'implies a more extensive process requiring relevant expertise and knowledge of standards, and following from the requirements and responsibilities of one's job. . . . Due care, objectivity and integrity arise from personal values and from society's expectations of professionalism' (CICA, 1988, p. 5). Taking these two explanations together, a definition of 'professional judgement in financial reporting' is 'judgment exercised with due care, objectivity and integrity within the framework provided by accounting and other applicable standards, by experienced and knowledgeable people on accounting and financial reporting issues arising in the preparation and issuance of financial statements, annual reports, prospectuses and similar documents' (CICA, 1988, p. 6). They offer a similar definition of professional judgment in the context of auditing in a later report. It is 'the application of relevant knowledge and experience, within the context provided by auditing and accounting standards and Rules of Professional Conduct, in reaching decisions where a choice must be made between alternative possible courses of action' (CICA, 1995, p. 5). This definition is followed by the IAASB (International Auditing and Assurance Standards Board) in *ISA 200* where professional judgement in auditing is defined as 'the application of relevant training, knowledge and experience, within the context provided by auditing, accounting and ethical standards, in making informed decisions about the courses of action that are appropriate in the circumstances of the audit engagement' (IAASB, 2010, *ISA 200*, §13 (k)).

These definitions bring out certain key elements of professional judgement that apply in the context of both financial reporting and auditing. Professional judgement has these characteristics:

i) a process that involves making choices or decisions about courses of action in a certain activity
ii) these choices or decisions are made in the context where there are standards to be followed
iii) such choices or decisions require certain skills, knowledge and experience to be used in making such decisions, and those making them have to exhibit certain qualities

It was suggested in chapter 2 that deciding to perform an intentional action—that is, decision-making—*is* coming to have a desire to act *as a result of reasoning*. The 'process' implied by the CICA definitions of 'professional judgement' is thus a process of reasoning to the desire to perform actions. The idea that decisions or choices need to be made in the context or framework of standards can be understood in two ways. The first way of understanding this relates to where a standard requires those who follow it to do something that involves making decisions or choices. An example in the financial reporting context would be where an accountant has to estimate the expected economic life of an asset where she is required by accounting standards to depreciate the asset. The kind of reasoning involved is inductive reasoning where a prediction of future economic life is derived from past experience of similar assets. This involves judgement since there is no necessity the asset will last a certain period of time given the inductive evidence. Some *decisions* or *choices* may need to be made in undertaking such reasoning (for example, the applicability of generalizations about similar kinds of assets and their relevance to the asset in question must be assessed; it may be important to look for other circumstances that may undermine the applicability of these generalizations to the case in question). These kinds of decisions would not need to be made where the standard said simply to depreciate the asset in question over, say, five years. From a requirement of this kind one can *deduce* the depreciation of the asset. Judgement is only involved where the reasoning to the action in question is *not deductive*. In the auditing context, standards may require the auditor to look for evidence to substantiate an assertion in the financial statements. Similarly, inductive reasoning rather than deductive reasoning is used in the search for evidence, and, as a result, judgement must be exercised.

The focus on professional judgement for much of the research concerns decisions or choices of this kind. Much of the empirical research on judgement examines how it is exercised in making decisions or choices in respect of actions required to be undertaken by standards. There is little discussion of what it is to exercise such judgement—that is, there is little in the way of conceptual enquiry into the nature of judgements of this kind. This kind of judgement is not explored in this book. It is not that it is unimportant. The point is that it has little to do with the nature of the accounting standards promulgated by standard setters and, hence, has little to do with the nature of accounting regulation. Any kind of standard may include a requirement to do something involving an exercise of judgement of this kind. Whether or not a standard includes such a requirement has nothing to do with whether it is 'rules-based' or 'principles-based' for example. The same cannot be said about the second way of understanding why decisions or choices may need to be made in following standards. Such decisions or choices arise because the action of following the standard itself, rather than undertaking another action required by the standard, may result in the need to make choices or decisions. This does have relevance to the question of the kind of standard promulgated.

ICAS appear to have this kind of judgement in mind in saying that 'rules-based' standards do not involve the exercise of professional judgement. The fact that they equate arguments for and against rules with arguments for or against 'rules-based' standards (ICAS, 2006, pp. 8–9) suggests they equate 'rules-based' standards with rules. Their definition of a rule makes this clear. It is 'a means of establishing an unambiguous decision-making method. There can be no doubt about when and how it is to be applied. Rules represent specific instructions—like a computer program' (ICAS, 2006, p. 8). There is no need to exercise judgement in complying with them, for there are no choices or decisions to be made. This is the characteristic of 'rules-based' standards. A similar picture of standards is given by the Fédération des Experts Comptables Européens (FEE). Judgement is not exercised where standards contain 'a definitive, comprehensive list of procedures (an algorithm)' (FEE, 2007, §34). Algorithms represent 'a finite set of instructions for performing a particular task' (FEE, 2007, §254). Where a standard expresses a rule, in the generic sense, and the rule is an algorithm then it appears to be the kind of rule identified by ICAS—that is, a 'rules-based' rule. Rules of this kind in standards are contrasted with 'principles-based' standards that require choices or decisions to be made in following them. A 'principle' is defined as 'a general statement, with widespread support, which is intended to support truth and fairness and acts as a guide to action. Principles cannot be replaced by mechanical rules' (ICAS, 2006, p. 4).

Another distinguishing factor of the two kinds of accounting standard is the extent to which exceptions are included in standards. 'Principles-based' standards 'minimize exceptions' (SEC, 2003, p. 5) whereas 'rule-based' standards 'contain numerous exceptions to the principles purportedly underlying the standards (SEC, 2003, p. 11). These two characteristics of kinds of accounting standard are connected. If exceptions are included in standards then the exercise of a certain kind of judgement in following standards is not required. Both characteristics represent different responses to the problem of what to do when a rule meant to achieve a certain objective will not achieve this objective in all circumstances where it is followed. One solution to this problem is to include exceptions to the general rule in the standard. Another solution is to allow the rule to be overridden in such circumstances. Whether one solution or the other is possible depends upon the particular conception of rules that is adopted by standard setters when they promulgate rules. The idea that there may be two conceptions of rules was suggested when the idea of a general rule from which specific rules can be derived was examined in chapter 3. The solution to the problem that a rule may not achieve an objective in all circumstances that allows the rule to be overridden in such circumstances conceives rules as 'rules of thumb'. The solution that builds exceptions into the rule often proceeds from conceiving rules as rules on the 'practice' conception. The debate between 'principles-based' and 'rules-based' standards starts from the wrong point. Instead of focusing on exceptions it should focus on the problem that exceptions are meant to address and on the conception of rules that makes the solution of including exceptions in rules useful or redundant. It is argued in this chapter that before a solution is adopted standard setters should decide upon the conception of rules they are to promulgate in accounting standards. It is argued that the conception of rules has been largely ignored by standard setters. One reason for not considering this matter is the inconvenience that arises for projects that seek to converge accounting standards when the standards being converged may contain rules that are conceived differently. It is questioned whether true convergence of standards is possible without agreement on the kind of rule to be expressed in converged standards. Before investigating the two solutions to the problem identified, including exceptions or allowing judgement to override the rule, another solution to the problem is considered, namely the solution that does not recognise the problem at all.

SEE NO EVIL . . .

The SEC place considerable faith in standard setters and their ability to promulgate standards in such a way that the problem of standards that do not fulfil desires on every occasion does not really exist. They argue that 'it is . . . precisely the role of the standard setter to define the class of transactions included within the economic arrangement and then to establish the appropriate accounting for that class of transactions. While not everyone will agree with the standard setter's conclusions, making the determination of the underlying economic of an arrangement and the appropriate accounting for that arrangement are integral to the standard setter's role' (SEC, 2003, p. 32). Few would disagree that it is the standard setter's job to determine the accounting that best fulfils the purpose of the rule. The point is whether the standard setter can be expected to establish a requirement for accounting that always fulfils the purpose. Is there always a rule that, if followed, will fulfil the purpose on all occasions? It has been suggested that the history of 'rules-based' standards belies the idea that standards 'can portray economic arrangements in a way that omits nothing of relevance to investors, creditors and other users, and can specify and effectively deal with how these should be accounted for'. This is an 'impossible dream' (Benston, Bromwich and Wagenhofer, 2006, p. 177). The assumption that there must always be a rule that always meets the objectives of financial reporting is just that—an assumption that may not be justified.

This is not really what the SEC is assuming, though. They state that they 'believe that when the standard setter establishes standards under an objectives-oriented regime, the accounting should, in virtually all cases, be consistent with the standard setter's view of the nature of the economic arrangement' (SEC, 2003, p. 32). The expression 'virtually all' recognises that there will be cases where the accounting is not appropriate. It is just that there should not be many such cases. The SEC's faith in the ability of the standard setter to determine what actions are appropriate in the many and varied circumstances that might arise may or may not be warranted given the history of standard setting. The question that follows is what to do when such cases arise.

One solution is simply not to worry about them. Standard setters may accept that following a rule on every occasion when it applies will not fulfil the objectives or desires which prompted its promulgation. It is acknowledged that the objectives or general desires that are used in promulgating standards will not be achieved *on all occasions* of following the rule. This would create a problem if the standard setter claims to want to achieve these desires on all occasions—that is, universally. Whether or not this is the case may depend upon the conception of a framework of desires, like that expressed in the conceptual framework, and whether or not these desires are meant to be universally or only generally desired. It is not such a problem if what is wanted is only wanted generally, for this allows that the desire may not necessarily be achieved on all occasions. The problem that desires may not always be met has been recognised in the auditing context. Auditing standards 'cannot represent a comprehensive list of audit procedures applicable in all circumstances. Such standards can contain a short list of audit procedures that are almost always necessary in most circumstances' (FEE, 2007, §268). This may be accepted, but if the standard setter still requires the rule to be followed on all occasions, even where it is clear following the rule will not achieve the desired ends, this seems to be somewhat perverse and might be seen to undermine the credibility of the rule. After all, if rules are seen as instrumental to achieving an end then if they do not achieve the end on a particular occasion surely there is no reason to follow them. It might be argued that more good is achieved by insisting the rule be followed on all occasions even if on some occasions it does not achieve the desired end than adopting some other solution to instances where the rule does not seem to work. Although this might be the case, and there may be arguments that can be made in its favour, adopting this solution without exploring whether there are other ways of dealing with this problem would seem precipitate. One possible solution to the problem would be to exclude the circumstances when following the rule would not achieve the general desires from the ambit of the rule. In other words, the rule that is promulgated may include *exceptions*.

EXCEPTIONS IN RULES

A rule that contains exceptions will be of the kind 'Do *A* except in circumstances *X*, *Y* and *Z*'. If there are many circumstances where following the rule will not achieve the objectives then there will be many exceptions in the rule. If there are too many exceptions then this calls into question whether the rule should have been promulgated in the first place. If a rule is supposed to achieve certain ends and it does not in many cases then promulgating the rule and excluding these cases seems pointless. A better rule should be sought that meets these desires at least more generally. The SEC acknowledges this when they observe that 'the existence of numerous exceptions to a standard are an indication that, either the underlying principle may not be appropriate, or the scope of the standard is too broad' (SEC, 2003, p. 62). The former problem is, presumably, that the desire that prompts the standard is not appropriate. The latter problem is, presumably, that the rule covers too many reporting circumstances to deal with under one rule.

The problem of including rules with exceptions, one of the criteria of 'rules-based' standards, is identified by the SEC. They observe that standards with many exceptions result in 'inconsistencies in accounting treatment of transactions and events with similar economic substance' (SEC, 2003, p. 11). This means that 'transactions that are substantively the same may receive very different accounting' and that 'comparability in reporting can be illusory' (SEC, 2003, p. 17). In effect, a consequence of this approach is to substitute one rule that applies in a range of circumstances with a number of rules that require different actions in different circumstances. It is no wonder that in characterizing 'rules-based' standards as those with exceptions the perception that such systems include a proliferation of rules develops. This may be embarrassing to the standard setters who must then offer a defence against the claim that this proliferation of rules results in different accounting treatments in circumstances that appear to be, in important respects, similar. The demand for comparability and consistency 'is the reason to have reporting standards' (Schipper, 2003, p. 62). If it is not achieved then something would appear to be wrong with the standards promulgated. The FASB and IASB explain that '*comparability* is the quality of information that enables users to identify similarities in and differences between two sets of economic phenomena. *Consistency* refers to the use of the same accounting policies and procedures, either from period to period within an entity or in a single period across entities. Comparability is the goal; consistency is a means to an end that helps in achieving that goal' (FASB/IASB, 2006, QC35). If information is comparable 'like things must look alike and different things must look different' (FASB/IASB, 2006, p. 31). If, through the use of exceptions in standards, the standard setter prescribes different accounting policies and procedures in the same or similar circumstances then comparability will not be achieved and the objectives of standard setting are frustrated.

A lot hangs on understanding what it means to say that the circumstances are the 'same', 'substantially the same' or 'similar'. Wittgenstein once said that 'the use of the word "rule" and the use of the word "same" are interwoven' (Wittgenstein, 1953, §225). In other words if the rule for the meaning of an expression allows a word to be applied in two circumstances then the circumstances *are* the same. If two things are the same this *means* that the same expression can be applied to both. As an example, if the expression 'university lecturer' is correctly applied to two people then they are the same. What makes them the *same* is not some underlying 'substance', but the fact that one expression is applied to both. Wittgenstein challenged the prevailing orthodoxy in philosophical circles that concepts are developed by noticing similarities and using a word to denote the resemblance. He reverses this process. Things are the same not because they have a resemblance but rather resemble each other because the same word is applied to them. It is important to see that the fact that the same expression is used in describing two people or things makes them the same but does not preclude the fact that they may also be different in so far as *another* expression might be applied to the one and not the other. For example, although two people may be the same in that they might both be university lecturers, one might be a man and the other a woman. In so far as an expression 'man' is applied to one and not to the other then they are also *different*.

Where there is a rule with an exception the intention is that the rule will be applied in certain circumstances but not where the circumstances described in the exception apply. The point is that the circumstance in which the rule applies is different from that in which the exception is applied. SFAS No. 133 is cited by the SEC as an example of a standard with exceptions. There are said to be 'nine exceptions to its scope' in paragraphs 10–11 (SEC, 2003, p. 23). Contracts that are not subject to the requirements of SFAS No. 133 include ' "Regular-way" security trades', 'Normal purchases and normal sales', 'Certain insurance contracts', 'Financial guarantee contracts', etc. The worry about these exceptions is whether the kind of transaction excluded from the ambit of the SFAS is different from the kind of derivative included in the ambit of the standard. The argument against this kind of rule is that the included and excluded transactions are similar or the same—that is, they have the 'same economic substance'. Given Wittgenstein's explanation of 'same', this only means that other descriptions may be applied to both kinds of transactions, the included and the excluded. In certain respects they are the same even if in other respects, namely in having the descriptions ' "Regular-way" security trades', 'Normal purchases and normal sales', etc. applied to them and not to derivatives covered by the SFAS, they are different. They are the same but also different.

The SEC does not actually say that the circumstances have the 'same economic substance', only that they have 'similar economic substance'. What this means is that, although not *all* of the same expressions are applied to both circumstances, *some* of them are applied to both. This makes them *similar*, but not the same. The fact that other descriptions are not applied to both makes them different. This is why the SEC talks about 'substantively the same'. The latter involves a *judgement* that the descriptions which make the two circumstances the same are *more important* than the descriptions which make them different. In other words, some decision or choice has to be made as to whether the descriptions that make them the same are more important than the descriptions that make them different. A number of descriptions might apply to both. Being 'substantively the same', having the 'same economic substance', may have nothing to do with the *number* of descriptions circumstances have in common. The point is that the ways in which they are similar are more *important* than the ways in which they are not. Whether or not the difference in circumstances is important depends upon whether applying the rule in the normal circumstances and applying it in the circumstances covered by the exception will result in the achievement of the objectives of the standard in both cases. The argument against exceptions is that if the rule is not followed in certain circumstances, because exceptions to these circumstances have been made in the rule, then the rule will not achieve these objectives.

Exceptions are included in a standard when the standard setter has decided that following the rule in the circumstances covered by an exception will not achieve the objectives of the rule. This decision is made by the standard setters given their grasp of the objectives of the standard and their belief that following the rule in these circumstances will not achieve the objectives of the rule. If the objectives of the rule are those set out in a conceptual framework for financial reporting then it is these objectives or desires that are considered when deciding whether the inclusion of the exception is desirable and the similarities more important than the differences. This is an exercise of *judgement* that is a result of the kind of practical reasoning undertaken by standard setters. The result may be a proliferation of rules where no judgement is allowed in deciding what to do and no choices or decisions are allowed or required to be made in following these rules. An alternative to the standard setters exercising judgement is for them to leave it to the accountant to decide to follow or not follow the rule in these circumstances.

THE ALTERNATIVE TO EXCEPTIONS

Allowing the accountant to override the rule—that is, to *exercise judgement* in deciding whether or not to follow the rule because it will not achieve the objectives of the rule—is to treat the rule as a 'rule of thumb'. Allowing the override and including exceptions are not necessarily mutually exclusive. If there are circumstances the standard setter is aware of where following the rule will not meet these ends or objectives she may well exclude them from the ambit of the rule even if she allows an override to deal with such circumstances. Where this is done the accountant does not need to exercise judgement in deciding on an override. This is done for them as the standard setter has decided or chosen to exclude such circumstances from the rule. She has exercised 'collective judgement' in reasoning from the desires and beliefs to the standard. Where there are circumstances where the override would be required on all or perhaps on many occasions then it would make sense to exclude those occasions from the ambit of the rule. The existence or not of exceptions thus does not coincide with a particular kind of rule. However, given this understanding of the role of exceptions, it is more likely that in a system of standards that does not allow an override—that is, where rules are conceived on the 'practice' conception—there are more exceptions than in a system that does allow an override. There is a link between the existence or otherwise of exceptions in an accounting system and the conception of rules that is adopted in such a system.

A system that adopts a conception of rules as 'rules of thumb' and allows an override would be likely to have standards with few exceptions. It would also be a system where judgement, at least judgement of a certain kind, had to be exercised in following the rules. If having few exceptions and exercising judgment are characteristics of 'principles-based' standards then a system which includes rules conceived as 'rules of thumb' might be characterized as 'principles-based'. A system that adopts a conception of rules as rules on the 'practice' conception without an override and hence without the need to exercise judgement of a certain kind would be more likely to have standards with exceptions. If having standards with exceptions where the exercise of judgement is not required is a characteristic of 'rules-based' standards then a system which includes rules conceived on the 'practice' conception might be characterized as 'rules-based'. The conception of rules adopted in a system is a more important determinant of the kind of system, 'principles-based' or 'rules-based', than is the presence or absence of exceptions. It is suggested that the presence or absence of exceptions is a *consequence* of the more important decision about the conception of the kind of rule that is to appear in standards. It is more sensible to characterize different kinds of standards in terms of the conception of rules that are adopted by standard setters. 'Principles-based' standards would then be characterized as standards where the rule in the standard is a 'rule of thumb'. The presence or absence of exceptions would not be a criterion of kinds of standards or systems of standards. There may be an empirical generalization to the effect that certain kinds of standards or systems of standard are more or less likely to include exceptions in standards, but having or not having exceptions is not a criterion of being a particular kind of standard or system of standards.

SYSTEMS OF STANDARDS AND THE CONCEPTION OF RULES

The link between the override and kinds of accounting system is made by some writers. It has been argued that a true and fair override is 'a necessary requirement for any standard setting approach', particularly a 'principles-based' approach, in order to 'avoid allowing or even requiring accountants to follow rules by letter but not by intention' (Benston, Bromwich and Wagenhofer, 2006, p. 167). It has been said that 'the true and fair view override is the cornerstone of professional judgment' (Bennett, Bradbury and Prangnell, 2006, p. 201). Alexander and Jermakowicz observe that 'recent signed editorials in *Abacus* (Dean and Clarke, 2004, 2005) have emphasized both the importance of the "true and fair view" and "principles v. rules" debates, and the close linkage between them' (Alexander and Jermakowicz, 2006, p. 132). One of these editorials states that 'the suggestion by many commentators . . . that the IFRS regime is principles- rather than rule-based . . . the general tenor of their comments gives reason to imagine that such a distinction is underpinned by the qualitative criterion, "true and fair view" (or its equivalent) legal or professional override' (Dean and Clarke, 2005, p. i). The idea of 'underpinning' could be interpreted to mean that the meaning of 'principles-based' includes the criterion of being a system that allows an override on 'true and fair view' grounds. This suggests that the 'close linkage' is a matter of meaning—that is, that being a 'principles-based' standard is being a standard that expresses 'rules of thumb', which implies an override is allowable.

In the UK the requirement of the Companies Acts to give a true and fair view of the state of affairs of the company may in special circumstances require a departure from accounting standards (Companies Act 1985, Sections 226(5) and 227(6)). This allows companies to override the rules in standards where following them will not result in a true and fair view. This suggests the UK is a system where rules are conceived of as 'rules of thumb'. The existence of the override in the UK was confirmed in a recent legal opinion given to the Financial Reporting Council (FRC). However, the idea of 'true and fair' now seems to be closely linked to achieving the objectives of the conceptual framework. The UK's conceptual framework was said to have 'the true and fair view concept at its foundation' (ASB, 1999, §13). This is because 'it is inherent in the nature of the true and fair view concept that financial statements will not give a true and fair view unless the information they contain is sufficient in quantity and quality to satisfy the reasonable expectations of the readers to who they are addressed' (ASB, 1999, §12). Given that the conceptual framework adopts a user needs approach and its 'principles' set out what is wanted and the qualities of useful information then it would seem at least a necessary condition of giving a 'true and fair view' that the 'principles' in the conceptual framework are achieved. The link between achieving the objectives in the conceptual framework and presenting a 'true and fair view' is made in the legal opinion given to the FRC where departure from both IFRS and UK accounting standards is allowed if they are 'so misleading that it would conflict with the objectives of the financial statements set out in the Framework' (Moore, 2008, §36). There is plenty of support in jurisdictions like the UK which allow this kind of departure for an override 'where GAAP does not allow firms to show their economic position' (Benston, Bromwich and Wagenhofer, 2006, p. 177).

Other participants in the debate about systems of standards do not make this connection. Schipper chooses not to discuss the 'true and fair override' in her discussion of 'principles-based' accounting standards. In the U.S. listed companies are required to 'present fairly' their results and financial position and the auditor's report includes the statement that the financial statement 'presents fairly'. Zeff (1990) argues that the idea of a 'true and fair view' is not the same as the U.S. 'presents fairly' in the auditor report. The words 'presents fairly' never stand alone but are always seen in conjunction with 'generally accepted accounting principles'. For this reason the 'TFV [true and fair view] legal requirement with its override implications has not been adopted in the U.S. regulatory system' (Alexander and Jermakowicz, 2006, p. 144). Rule 203 of the AICPA Code of Professional Conduct allows departure from GAAP in 'unusual circumstances' and says that it 'is a matter of professional judgment' to determine what circumstances warrant such a departure (Alexander and Jermakowicz, 2006, p. 145). However, van Hulle noted that 'the representative of the SEC argued that—although there is an override test in the auditing standards in the US—no registrant with the SEC had ever applied the override in its financial statements' (van Hulle, 1997, p. 718; also quoted in Alexander and Jermakowicz, 2006, p. 145). In effect, there is no override of accounting standards in the U.S. This suggests that rules are conceived on the 'practice' conception. In so far as the U.S. system moves to a 'principles-based' system at least some commentators do not believe this implies that rules in standards are 'rules of thumb'. The SEC also rejects the view that 'a necessary component of principles-based standards is the inclusion of a "true and fair override" ' (SEC, 2003, p. 32). The idea of standards being 'principles-based' is not for them a matter of the standards including 'rules of thumb' for which an override is allowable.

The position with respect to international accounting standards and to jurisdictions applying them in the EU is not so clear cut. Although there is a similar override in the Fourth Directive of the EU and an override is allowed in IAS 1 it is not clear whether this is interpreted as similar to the UK's override or closer to the U.S. position. It has been suggested that it is likely to be interpreted differently in different jurisdictions within the EU and by those who follow international accounting standards (Evans, 2003). It is thus unclear whether accounting standards as conceived by the IASB and adopted by the EU include 'rules of thumb' or rules on the 'practice' conception. Given that international standards are said to be 'principles-based' it is not clear whether this implies that judgement can be exercised in overriding them in certain circumstances or whether this kind of judgement is precluded. It is not also not clear whether international standards are conceived as standards expressing 'rules of thumb' or as rules on the 'practice' conception. What are the implications for the idea of standards as 'principles-based'?

'PRINCIPLES-BASED' STANDARDS

There appears to be a consensus amongst standard setters like the ASB, the FASB and the IASB that standards should be 'principles-based'. As noted earlier, one of the criteria for being a standard that is 'principles-based' is that it should contain 'few, if any, exceptions' (SEC, 2003, p. 12). What appears mysterious is how standard setters can agree upon the kind of standard that should be promulgated when they may start from very different conceptions of the rules expressed by them.

A standard setter like the ASB that operates in a jurisdiction where an override is allowed conceives rules as 'rules of thumb'. If a rule can be overridden when it does not meet certain objectives such as giving a 'true and fair view' or following the principles in the conceptual framework then there is little pressure to include exceptions in the rules expressed in standards. The rule will be overridden if this is the case and if those following the rule think the consequences of following or not following the rule are important. If following a rule in certain circumstances will not achieve the ends then it need not be followed. The circumstances need not be excluded from the ambit of the rule by the use of exceptions. Given the override the ASB can readily agree that standards should be 'principles-based' and should include 'few, if any, exceptions'.

The situation is rather different for the FASB. If there is no effective override and rules are conceived on the 'practice' conception then what do they do if following a rule in certain circumstances will not meet the objectives of the rule? One response would be to include exceptions in such circumstances. If there are a lot of circumstances where this might happen there would be a lot of exceptions to the rule. The rule would become, in the jargon, 'rules-based'. If such standards and the exceptions that go with them are eschewed then what can the standard setter do? Two responses have been considered previously. The first is to maintain that this will not happen since the standard setter's role is to choose standards that meet the objectives in 'virtually all cases'. Whether or not this is possible depends upon how the history of standard setting is read. As noted earlier, some writers suggest this is an impossible dream. Another response is to admit that standards may not meet the objectives in all cases but not worry about such cases if most of the time the objectives are met. The consequences of following or not following the rule in the circumstances may not be deemed important. If either of these responses are made by standard setters then they might well accept that standards should be 'principles-based' and hence should include 'few, if any, exceptions'.

Both kinds of standard setters might agree on 'principles-based' standards as having this characteristic, but their seeming agreement may mask important disagreements. A standard setter in a jurisdiction that enjoys an override may believe that a rule in a standard will not meet the objectives in all circumstances and that this is important but may accept the standard because he knows the rule can be overridden in circumstances where it will not meet the objectives. A standard setter in a jurisdiction that does not enjoy the override may believe the rule in a standard will meet the objectives in all circumstances and accepts the standard. Alternatively, he may believe that it will not but that this is not important. In either of these cases there are significant disagreements with the first standard setter, but there can nonetheless be agreement on the standard.

It will not matter much to the IASB which of these kinds of jurisdictions their standards are to operate within or what beliefs underlie acceptance of the standard. Rules with 'few, if any, exceptions' can be promulgated and accepted. In this happy position there can be convergence on standards and also a belief that a certain kind of standard, 'principles-based' standards defined as those with 'few, if any, exceptions', is preferable. The trouble is that the 'convergence' is only skin deep. What happens if circumstances arise where following the rule in the standard will not meet the objectives of the rule? In the jurisdiction with an override where it is believed to be important if the objectives of the rule are not met in the circumstances, the rule will not be followed. In the jurisdiction without an override the rule will be followed and justified on the grounds that, in reality, following the rule will meet the objectives since, if it was not the case, the standard setter would not have promulgated it, or that even if it does not this does not matter so long as following the rule, in general, will achieve the objectives. Different accounting will occur in the two jurisdictions. Financial statements will not be comparable because the accounting treatments are not consistent. One of the enhancing qualitative characteristics in the conceptual framework is not met. Financial reporting has not converged even if there is apparent convergence on not only the rules but also the kind of rules that should be promulgated in standards.

In order to achieve real convergence it seems clear that the issue of the override—and any beliefs about whether it is possible to promulgate rules that will achieve the objectives of the rules in all or most circumstances and whether or not it matters if there are circumstances where following the rule will not achieve these ends—should have been discussed and agreed upon before any convergence project went very far. This does not appear to have happened. The issue of the override was sidelined, and there was little discussion of the underlying beliefs about rules and the consequences of following them. It is not surprising that this did not happen in the light of the commitment to convergence of accounting standards by the FASB and the IASB.

THE CONVERGENCE PROJECT AND THE AMBIGUITY ABOUT KINDS OF RULES

As part of the fallout of the Enron debacle the Sarbanes-Oxley Act directed the SEC to conduct a study on the adoption of a 'principles-based accounting system'. As a result of the study the SEC recommended that the standard setting process should develop 'principles-based' standards. The FASB agree with the recommendations of the SEC study. They noted that the SEC has observed 'a continuing shift by the FASB towards a more objectives-oriented regime should facilitate the convergence process' (FASB, 2004, p. 10). Before this statement was made the FASB had signed the Norwalk Agreement, which committed the FASB to working towards convergence of accounting standards with the IASB.

Adopting a 'principles-based' system does facilitate convergence if the criteria adopted do not require a fundamental change to how accounting standards are conceived. This has been achieved by defining standards of this kind as those with 'few, if any, exceptions' without adjudicating on the conception of rules in standards. If a 'principles-based' system implied the adoption of standards that are 'rules of thumb' which allow an override then the FASB would have committed itself to changing the kind of rules expressed in their standards. It would have meant that U.S. standards, conceived on the 'practice' conception, would have to be abandoned. A convenient way of escaping this consequence was to avoid defining 'principles-based' standards as standards that include 'rules of thumb' with an attendant override. In effect this is what the FASB have done. The IASB have followed suit for the same reason. 'Principles-based' standards are defined by other criteria, including the criteria relating to exceptions. The discussion of the kind of rule expressed in accounting standards has been simply ignored in order to smooth the road to convergence. If convergence is achieved it will be 'on the cheap'. A rearguard action is being fought by some accounting academics who have suggested that the idea of a 'principles-based' standard might imply standards that contain rules of a certain kind.

IMPLICATIONS FOR THE STANDARD SETTER

It was suggested that a certain combination of conceptions is problematic. If a standard setter conceives of desires as universal so that they can be used in deducing standards then no judgement needs to be exercised by the standard setter in adjudicating amongst desires in making standard setting decisions. However, if this is done then either exceptions have to be included in rules or an override has to be allowed. If an override is allowed then judgement has to be exercised by those who follow standards. If no override is allowed then exceptions are the only way to deal with the problem. A standard setting position that takes desires as universal and takes rules as on the 'practice' conception can only deal with the problem that rules may not achieve the objectives on all occasions by including exceptions. If 'principles-based' standards are those standards that do not include many exceptions then such a regime cannot accept such standards. They are forced down the route of 'rules-based' standards. Arguably, this is exactly the position in the U.S. They appear to conceive a conceptual framework as something to be used in the deduction of standards. This means the desires in the framework need to be universal. This means they cannot accept 'principles-based' standards without allowing an override. As no override is allowed in U.S. standards, in effect, standard setters must include exceptions to deal with the problem. If 'principles-based' standards exclude exceptions then they cannot accept such standards. The desire to promulgate 'principles-based' standards must result in incoherence given the conception of objectives and of rules.

This analysis suggests it is more important to decide on the conception of rules in accounting standards than to decide whether to promulgate rules that are 'principles-based' and do not contain many exceptions or to promulgate rules that are 'rules-based' and contain a number of exceptions. The inclusion or otherwise of exceptions is a consequence of a decision about the conception of rules in standards. The characteristic of the presence or absence of exceptions that is used to distinguish kinds of standard is something of an epiphenomenon that obscures a more important underlying issue. A more useful way of distinguishing kinds of accounting standard is to use the criterion of the conception of rules in standards. This would force standard setters to focus on the question of how they conceive of rules in standards and hence on the question of whether or not an override is to be allowed in following such standards. This conclusion supports the rearguard action of those academics who argue for the importance of discussing the override in the debates about the ideal kind of standard. The reluctance of the FASB and SEC to engage in this discussion is a mistake. It is necessary for standard setters to consider the important question of the conception of rules in standards and the consequences of adopting different conceptions into the debate.

Although the neglect of the question of the conception of rules in accounting standards is understandable, it is difficult to believe that true convergence on standards is really possible when the conception of rules in accounting systems that are supposed to be converging may be different. Any 'convergence' of rules that are conceived differently is a 'fudge' and does not represent true convergence. It seems an obvious point to make that before a project of convergence takes place there should be some discussion and agreement about the kind of rules that are to be included in standards. The commitment to 'due process' in the development of International Financial Reporting Standards (IFRSs) as well as in the development of interpretations of IFRSs is announced in the *Preface to IFRSs* (IASB, 2010, A18). It is strange that there is no discussion, and a fortiori no due process, relating to the decision or choice of the kind of standards that are to appear in accounting standards. As suggested earlier, the reason for this can be understood, but that does not really amount to an excuse for not considering the question. The ambiguity in the idea of a 'principles-based' standard and the consequent lack of agreement about the kind of rule that exists in accounting standards does 'serve a purpose' (Page and Spira, 2005, p. 301). This is an explanation but not an excuse.

It is suggested that now is the time to look more closely at accounting standards and the question of the conception of rules they express. This will also involve revisiting the question of whether or not an override of standards should be allowed. These questions should be at the centre of debates about the ideal kind of standard. This will sideline the artificial debate about 'principles-based' versus 'rules-based' standards, which serves only to divert attention from providing answers to these important questions.

SUMMARY

This chapter considers possible responses of standard setters to the problem of what to do about prospective rules setting out requirements of financial reporting that do not meet the objectives that underlie the decision to promulgate standards on all occasions when they are to be followed. If the problem is recognised to be important, two main solutions that might be adopted involve the exercise of judgement. The idea of judgement is examined in a conceptual enquiry into its nature. It is suggested that judgement arises when the reasoning to decisions about what to do is not deductive. The first solution is to include exceptions in the standard that exclude from the ambit of the rule the necessity to follow the requirements in certain circumstances. This outcome is the result of an exercise of judgement *by standard setters* who consider in what circumstances the objectives of the standard are met by following the rule and those where they will not be met. This has been said to reduce comparability through a failure of consistency. An alternative solution is to allow those who follow the standards to override the requirement in circumstances where following it will not achieve the objectives of the *standard*. This outcome is the result of an exercise of judgement *by those who follow the rule*. Allowing an override depends upon accepting rules in standards as 'rules of thumb' rather than as rules on the 'practice' conception. Whether or not an override is allowed and whether or not the alternative of including exceptions in standards might be viewed as characteristics that distinguish 'rules-based' from 'principles-based' standards. It is suggested that the project to converge accounting standards needs to consider the conception of rules in standards before true convergence is possible.

5   The Nature and Role of Explanatory Guidance in Accounting Standards

In the previous chapter the exercise of judgement in making decisions or choices in the action of following the standard itself, rather than undertaking another action required by the standard, was examined. Judgement may need to be exercised where rules are conceived as 'rules of thumb', and the accountant following those rules needs to decide whether to follow the rule on a particular occasion or to override the rule if it does not meet the objectives of the rule. In this chapter another kind of judgement that may arise in relation to the action of following a standard is examined. It considers the exercise of judgement in *interpreting standards*. The kinds of decisions and choices that need to be made concerning the action of following the standard and the kind of reasoning that is used in making decisions about the course of action are examined. This, again, throws light on the distinction between 'rules-based' and 'principles-based' standards.

The CICA report *Professional Judgement in Financial Reporting* suggests that 'considerable judgment is needed in interpreting and applying . . . standards, sometimes because the standards are not fully consistent, clear, comprehensive or up to date' (CICA, 1988, p. 131). This exercise of judgement was recognised in two of the five categories of judgement identified in the CICA report. Of the 216 items of judgement examined in U.S. accounting pronouncements, either APB Opinions or FASB Statements, 187 related to the exercise of judgement in interpreting standards (Mason and Gibbins, 1991). 'Semantic judgement'—that is, judgement about the meaning of words which would seem to involve interpretation—is identified as one of the three kinds of judgement to be exercised in applying 'incomplete' accounting standards. It is needed because accounting expressions or 'concepts' used in such standards are 'vague' (Brown, Collins and Thornton, 1993, p. 281). The AAA Financial Accounting Standards Committee encouraged the FASB to emphasise the use of judgment in interpreting and implementing 'concepts-based standards' (AAA, 2003, p. 81). This kind of judgement has been relatively neglected in recent discussions. The exercise of judgement in interpreting accounting standards is not one of the categories of judgement in preparing financial statements explicitly identified in the ACIFR *Report*. This is surprising given the previous interest in this kind of judgement.

This chapter will clarify the nature of this kind of judgement and show that it is important for standard setters to understand these kinds of judgement-making decisions about accounting standards. It examines the idea that accounting standards include rules and that these need to be interpreted by preparers. The need for interpretation arises out of the fact that standards are expressed in language. One reason given for the need to interpret standards is that the standard is expressed in language that is vague. This contention is examined using the ideas about the philosophy of language developed by Wittgenstein. The argument that *all* language is vague is considered. This argument is distinguished from another that suggests that language does not have determinacy of sense. The implications of both these arguments for the development of accounting standards and for the need for implementation guidance and the exercise of judgement in following standards are drawn out. As will become clear, both the nature of judgement in general and of judgement in the interpretation of standards in particular are not well understood. The implications for developing different kinds of accounting standards, whether 'rules-based' or 'principles-based', are considered. An interdisciplinary approach is adopted that uses insights from the philosophy of language and from the legal literature to throw a new light on the distinction between two kinds of standard.

Although the exercise of judgement is important in financial reporting it is surprising to find that very little has been written about the meaning of the expression 'judgement'. In other words, there has been little in the way of conceptual enquiry into judgement. A search of the accounting literature in 1991 revealed that although there were 939 references to judgement 'none of these references . . . explain what is meant by judgement' (Mason and Gibbins, 1991, p. 21). The CICA report did something to rectify this omission. Their definition of 'judgement', and of what is meant by 'professional' judgment, was considered in previous chapters. These definitions could be slightly adapted and used to define 'professional judgement in financial reporting' as 'the application of relevant knowledge and experience, within the context provided by accounting standards, in reaching decisions where a choice must be made between alternative possible courses of action'. The Fédérations des Experts Comptables Européens criticizes definitions of this kind because they refer to both application, understood as a process of some kind, and the outcomes of the process, the decision about or choice of a course of action. It also points out that they do not differentiate between the application of judgement and 'other kinds of decision-making, including guessing' (FEE, 2007, p. 79). A more fundamental objection to this kind of definition is that it is not clear what is meant by an 'application' or what kind of 'process' is involved. One way to deal with both these points is to say, as was suggested in chapter 3, that the exercise of judgement involves a 'process' or 'application' of *reasoning* in reaching a conclusion about what to do in financial reporting or auditing. This is different from guessing about what to do as the latter does not involve reasoning. Given this clarification it can be seen that it is important to describe the *kind of reasoning* involved. The common characteristic of the exercise of judgment considered at various points in this book is that it involves reasoning that is *not deductive*. Given the characteristics of such inference already considered, with deductive inference there is no question of having to make any choices or decisions in drawing conclusions from premises, for the conclusion is implicit in the premises and thus follows necessarily. If this is the case then such reasoning cannot involve *judgement*, for there are no choices or decisions to be made. This suggests a connection between the exercise of judgement and reasoning. *Judgement is exercised only when the reasoning involved in its exercise is not deductive.*

The FEE's own suggestion about the meaning of 'professional judgement' is that it should be described as 'the application of professional expertise in decision-making about alternative courses of action in the exercise of professional activities when such decision-making is not susceptible to algorithmic resolution' (FEE, 2007, p. 79). An algorithm is 'a definitive, comprehensive list of procedures' (FEE, 2007, p. 14) that represents 'a finite set of instructions for performing a particular task' (FEE, 2007, p. 79). Both financial reporting standards and auditing standards are said not to include algorithms because 'all require significant interpretation and therefore the application of significant expertise' (FEE, 2007, p. 88). An 'informal' definition of 'algorithm' is 'a set of rules that precisely defines a sequence of operations' that specifies 'the way it applies in all possible circumstances that could arise' and is hence 'controlled logical deduction'(Wikipedia, 2011). If standards are algorithms then it is possible to *deduce* what to do in all situations to which the requirement applies. Algorithms enable making deductions about what to do and thus involve no choices or decisions about what to do. There is no need to exercise judgement in order to determine what to do. One simply deduces what is to be done from the algorithm. Why is it not possible to deduce what to do with all standards? Why do some need to be interpreted and some kind of judgement exercised in following them?

THE NEED TO INTERPRET THE REQUIREMENTS IN STANDARDS

To interpret something is 'to explain the meaning of, to elucidate, unfold, show the purport of' (*Chambers Twentieth Century Dictionary 1971*). If the requirements in standards need to be interpreted then there is a need for some grasp of meaning before the requirements in a standard can be met. The requirements in a standard constitute a *rule* that needs to be followed. In this sense a 'rule' means a 'command to perform a certain action when certain conditions apply' (FEE, 2007, p. 79). This ties in with the concept of a rule in the legal literature considered in chapter 2. Rules are differentiated from singular commands by their *generality*. As the FEE suggest, if standards contain commands they are meant to apply *whenever certain conditions apply*. They do not apply on only one particular occasion.

One problem with promulgating rules, whether in the law or in accounting standards, arises from the obvious fact that they are expressed in *language*. In the legal context language is recognised as 'the main, but not the only, medium for communicators of rules' (Twining and Miers, 1976, p. 119). In order to understand the rule to be followed the language in which the rule is expressed must be understood. An important distinction needs to be made between the rule and the rule-formulation (Baker and Hacker, 1985, p. 41). A rule-formulation is just a string of words of the kind that appear in a statute or in an accounting standard. The rule is what is *understood* in understanding the meaning of the words in the rule-formulation. In order to follow a rule the rule must be grasped, which is done by understanding the meaning of the expressions in the rule-formulation. To grasp a rule and be able to follow it '*is* to know what acts accord with it and what violate it', for 'to be ignorant or mistaken about what acts are in accord with it is to be ignorant or mistaken about what the rule is' (Baker and Hacker, 1985, p. 97). If two people follow the same rule then they do the same thing in the same circumstances. Two people might understand the meaning of the expressions in the rule-formulation differently and hence not grasp the same rule. If this is the case then one should say that there is one *rule-formulation* but *two rules* (Baker and Hacker, 1985, ch. 3). Another description of what is happening is that two people have *interpreted* the rule-formulation in different ways. Where two people interpret the expressions differently they are not interpreting the rule differently, but they are interpreting the rule-formulation differently and concluding that it expresses different rules. Describing what is happening as 'interpreting a rule in different ways' is misleading, for it makes it appear it is the rule that is interpreted differently. In fact, it is the rule-formulation that is interpreted differently and not the rule. If two people are following the same rule then they do the same thing in the same circumstances. This is what following the same rule *means*. If they do different things then they are following different rules. Whether or not one of them is correct and the other not correct depends upon the *practice* of following a rule expressed in a rule-formulation. If there is an *agreed* practice in understanding the meaning of expressions in the rule-formulation this determines whether or not someone is interpreting a rule-formulation correctly (Baker and Hacker, 1985, ch. 4).

Problems may arise in determining what the rule *is* because the rule-formulation uses language, and language is 'an imperfect instrument which is often imperfectly used' (Twining and Miers, 1976, p. 119).

PROBLEMS WITH LANGUAGE

One problem with language is that different people may understand the expressions in the rule-formulation differently. This may be because they are ignorant about the meaning of these expressions. They may think that they mean one thing but the practice of using these expressions determines that they mean something else. Such ignorance can be overcome through explaining the meaning of the expressions. This reveals *what* rule is expressed in the rule-formulation. Explanations of this kind can be set out in *implementation guidance* in standards. The purpose of such guidance is thus *educational*: it explains the meaning of expressions in the rule-formulation to someone who does not know what they mean. These explanations draw upon the agreed practice in the use of these expressions. Grasping this should ensure that anyone following the rule will accord with the agreed practice of following the rule because they grasp the meaning of expressions in the rule-formulation and, hence, grasp what the rule *is*. Someone who has grasped the rule can explain the expressions in the rule-formulation in the same way as others who use the expressions in accordance with the practice *and* follows the rule in accordance with the agreed practice (Baker and Hacker, 1985, ch. 5). If the former is the case but the latter is not then this shows they have not *understood* the explanation they have given correctly.

It is important to see that the rule-formulation and the implementation guidance *together* determine the rule in the standard. This would be quite obvious if a rule was formulated using an expression where there was *no* practice of using an expression in a rule or the practice was not known to those attempting to follow the rule. If a rule in a standard said 'When producing financial statements you are required to gronk' it is unlikely anyone would know how to follow this rule. If 'implementation guidance' was provided that said 'to gronk is to draft an income statement and statement of financial position' then the rule would be understood as 'When producing financial statements you are required to draft an income statement and statement of financial position'. The rule is determined by the rule-formulation in conjunction with the implementation guidance.

Another problem with language arises where there is *no agreed practice* in the use of expressions in the rule-formulation. This means the expressions are *vague*. An expression is 'vague' if there is, 'in the practice of its application, significant disagreements about what uses of it are correct' (Baker and Hacker, 1980, p. 218). This means the rule expressed in the rule-formulation is not clear and there may be different interpretations of what the rule expressed in the rule-formulation actually is. This manifests itself in either or both the criteria for agreeing on the rule expressed in the rule-formulation noted earlier. There may be disagreements that become evident if the rule-formulation is not explained in the same way. There may be disagreements in the explanation of what is in accord with the rule. Disagreements may also become evident where the rule is followed differently. Preparers who follow rules in accounting standards may explain the rule differently, but this is not always evident, for their explanations are not normally in the public arena. What is more evident is where they follow the rule differently. It was noted earlier that this might be the result of ignorance of the meaning of the expressions in the rule-formulation. It might also be because the rule in the standard is vague. Saying that the rule is vague is really shorthand for saying that the expressions in the rule-formulation are vague. This results in there being no agreement about what the rule is.

In the legal literature it has been said that the fact that words are vague is a major problem a rule-maker faces (Twining and Miers, 1976, p. 122). Where there are different practices in using expressions in rule-formulations in accounting standards then the standard setter is faced with the problem that different preparers may think the standard expresses different rules. This is also a problem for the auditors who have to give an opinion on financial statements that is based on, amongst other things, an evaluation of management's judgments in applying the entity's applicable financial reporting framework. They need to determine whether the interpretation of the rule-formulation is acceptable. It seems an obvious point to make that rule-formulations cannot be interpreted in *any* way. It is not usually the case that there is *no practice* in understanding and using the expressions in the rule-formulation. If this were the case then there would be *no meaning* for those expressions and the rule-formulation would not express a rule. It is unlikely anyone would suggest that standard setters or legislators formulate rules in accounting standards using language that has *no* meaning. It is unlikely standard setters or preparers and auditors interpret rule-formulations in any way they like. Given that there is an existing practice in using the expressions—that is, there may be conventions that determine acceptable uses—this practice will constrain their interpretation. However, some *choice or decision* may need to be made where there are *different* practices of explaining the expressions, different conventions, in the rule-formulation and hence different rules as expressed in the rule-formulation. This choice or decision can be left to the practitioner, or it can be made by the standard setter.

If standard setters make this choice then one way of indicating their preferred meaning is to set out the meaning to be attributed to expressions in the rule-formulations in the standard using *implementation guidance*. It is important to understand what is being done if this strategy is adopted. This is not an educational device of the kind described earlier for informing preparers and auditors about the meaning of expressions of which they are ignorant. Its purpose is to *determine what rule is expressed by the rule-formulation*. The rule is what is expressed by the rule-formulation together with the implementation guidance. Determining what the rule *is to be* involves a choice between different practices in the use of expressions where there are different practices that are not agreed upon. In making such a choice the standard setter reasons in the same way she reasons when promulgating a rule in an accounting standard. This is the kind of 'means-end' or 'instrumental' reasoning or 'practical' reasoning described in chapter 2. Given that the conclusion does not follow deductively with the kind of necessity that characterizes deductive reasoning, drawing a conclusion in practical reasoning involves some element of *choice or decision*. This is because such reasoning is 'ampliative'—that is, the conclusion goes beyond the content of the premises. Because some decision is involved, reasoning of this kind can be said to involve an exercise of judgement. The question is 'Who exercises this judgement?'

Standard setters can exercise such judgement in deciding how the standard is to be interpreted and then indicate this by including implementation guidance in the standard. This judgement might be referred to as the 'collective judgement' (Skinner, 1995/2005, p. 147) of standard setters. If it is left to preparers rather than standard setters to decide amongst different practices in the use of expressions in the rule-formulation, guided by the conventional practices that may exist amongst preparers and users, then they will need to identify the relevant desires or objectives that constitute premises in reasoning towards a desire to interpret the rule-formulation in a certain way. The objectives the preparers should start with in reasoning would be the same kinds of desires that prompt the standard setter to promulgate a standard. The standard setter starts with desires expressed by a conceptual framework. This sets out the objectives of financial reporting, and this not only is used in reasoning to rules in standards, but it also acts as reasons for deciding to interpret the meaning of an expression in a rule.

It is important to see that not only rules develop from a consideration of the objectives of accounting, but also the very concepts we use also develop as ways of meeting these objectives. This is what has been called a 'naturalistic' view of language. This asserts that 'our language develops over millennia to fit our needs. As something arises that we need to mark off, so we develop, by a linguistic reflex, as it were, a way of marking it off. To mark distinctions that it seemed important to us to make. It follows, that to understand the meaning of any term is to understand those human interests, needs and practices in the context of which it arose and into which it fits' (Lyas, 1993, p. 163). In this context it means to understand the objectives of financial reporting. The definitions of the elements of financial statements are, themselves, expressions of concepts understood as the meaning of expressions. The elements are defined in the way they are as these concepts are thought to be useful in meeting the ends or objectives of financial statements. When expressions in rule-formulations are interpreted the same kind of reasoning from objectives to concepts like the elements also is undertaken.

If the standard setter does not undertake this reasoning the preparer starts with the same desires as expressed by the conceptual framework and then decides how to interpret the expressions in the rule-formulation. This suggests the conceptual framework is not just for standard setters as is sometime implied by those who formulate this framework (FASB/IASB, 2005, p. 1). 'Principles-based' standards are supposed to include a statement of the objective of the standard (SEC, 2003, p. 5). This is because the preparer, the person following the rule, needs to exercise judgement in interpreting the requirements in standards using the objective or desire as a premise in their reasoning to an interpretation of the standard—that is, towards determining what rule is to be expressed by the rule-formulation. This objective is presumably derived from the conceptual framework. 'Principles-based' standards are supposed to be 'based on an improved and consistently applied conceptual framework' (SEC, 2003, p. 5). What is shown here is that it is not just standard setters who 'base' standards on a conceptual framework. Preparers also 'base' their interpretation of standards on such a framework.

Although a decision is required about what rule is expressed in the standard where there are disagreements in the practice of using expressions in rule-formulations, it is not necessarily the case that *all* standards are vague. If there is an agreed practice of using expressions in rule-formulations in standards then there is no need for either the standard setter or the preparer to make a decision or choice about the rule in the standard. The rule is clear because there is an *agreed practice*. There is no need to interpret the standard, and no judgement in interpreting the standard needs to be exercised. Such standards do not have to have at least some of the characteristics of 'principles-based' standards. There is no need to include the objectives of the standards to assist the preparer in making a decision or choice, for there is no decision or choice. The SEC suggests that this is characteristic of such standards (SEC, 2003). There is also no need for interpretation or the exercise of judgement, as the ICAS suggest is characteristic of such standards (ICAS, 2006). If *all language is vague*, though, then it follows that all standards should have these characteristics. Is all language vague, though?

IS ALL LANGUAGE VAGUE?

The idea that all language is vague has some currency in the accounting literature (Brown, Collins and Thornton, 1993). It is argued that the 'analytic tradition' in philosophy aims at identifying the 'essence' of things. The essence of something is given in a definition that sets out the necessary and sufficient conditions for applying an expression to something. Everything denoted by an expression must have certain properties (necessary conditions), and if something has such conditions it comes under the expression (sufficient conditions). Wittgenstein is attributed with the insight that not all things have 'essences' because not all expressions have definitions of this kind. Language and following the rules of language in consequence involve an 'ineliminable element of judgment' (Brown, Collins and Thornton, 1993, p. 280). What implications does this have for rules of accounting in standards?

Take a rule which says 'report assets'. If there is a definition that sets out the necessary and sufficient conditions of being an 'asset' then no judgement is required in following the rule. If something has all the sufficient conditions then it is an asset and must be reported. If it has each of the necessary conditions then it is an asset and needs to be reported. There are no choices or decisions to be made in 'interpreting' the rule, for what is required to report assets is given by the necessary conditions, and if something meets the sufficient conditions then it must be reported. No judgement is required because 'if all conditions were met accountants would know for certain that the item was an asset. If at least one condition were not met they could say for certain that the item was not an asset' (Brown, Collins and Thornton, 1993, p. 282). The reason for this certainty is that given the presence or absence of conditions the accountant can *deduce* that something was or was not an asset and did or did not need to be reported.

The FEE talks about the necessity to use judgement when an 'algorithmic resolution' is not possible. This only means that what is required by the rule cannot be deduced from the rule and the requisite definitions. If definitions have necessary and sufficient conditions 'the determination of whether the conditions for when the rules become relevant or the determination of how the action commanded by the rule ought to be carried out in detail' does not require 'significant interpretation'. This is because 'the content of the response and the circumstances can be defined in a precise manner'. In other words, a rule expressed in such language operates like an algorithm—that is, 'a definitive, comprehensive list of procedures' (FEE, 2007, §34) that follow deductively from the meaning of the expressions in the rule-formulation. With language that has such definitions there is no need to exercise judgement in interpreting the rule, for what to do in order to follow the rule can be deduced from the rule and the requisite definitions. It is also possible to deduce when a rule applies in the circumstance of a client. Brown, Collins and Thornton appear to equate the absence of necessary and sufficient conditions with vagueness. If a definition does set out such conditions then vagueness *may* be eliminated. Such definitions allow certain deductions to be made. Failure to make these deductions shows that the expression is misunderstood. All those who understand the expression correctly *must* arrive at the same conclusions about what does or does not come under an asset. They *must* agree on the practice of using the expression. If they do agree then the expression is not vague.

If an explanation of the meaning of an expression is not of this kind this does not mean it is vague, though. It may be that people agree on the use of an expression and, hence, it is not vague. Examples of explanation that are not of the preferred kind are given by Wittgenstein. They include explanations by giving an example of the kind of thing denoted by an expression, explanation by enumeration or explanation by criteria which might be called 'presumptive grounds' for the ascription of an expression to something that is defeasible in the light of countervailing evidence. Some expressions denote things that have a 'family resemblance' with other things that come under the expression. One thing may resemble another thing in respect of certain characteristics, but different things may resemble each other in different characteristics. This is similar to the way in which one member of a family resembles another. Some may have similar hair and eye colour whereas others are similar in respect to the shape of the nose or complexion. There may be no set of characteristics that *all* members of the family share and which determines that they belong to the same family (Dennis, 2008, p. 262).

One example of an explanation suggested by Wittgenstein is one that involves enumeration. An expression 'X' may be explained as 'either a or b or c'. An 'asset' might be defined as 'either goodwill or property, plant and equipment or debtors'. If there is a rule 'report assets' then given this kind of explanation someone can deduce 'report either goodwill or property, plant and equipment or debtors'. Someone might follow the rule by reporting goodwill. Another might follow it by reporting property, plant and equipment and yet another by reporting debtors. Some choice or decision would be required. In other words, judgement would need to be exercised. This is because from an explanation of the meaning of the expression 'asset' as 'either goodwill or property, plant and equipment or debtors' and the rule 'report assets', anyone following would have to make a decision about what to do. Different people could follow the rule even if they ended up doing different things. Similarly, with a 'family resemblance' such as the concept of 'game' it would be possible to follow the rule 'play a game' by playing chess, cards, rounders, hide and seek, etc. All count as games, and playing any one of them counts as following the rule. Does this mean the concept is vague? Everyone might agree on the explanation of the meaning of the expression, and everyone might agree the various actions were all instances of following the rule. There would be an agreement in practice on the use of the expression, and, hence, it would not be vague. Anyone following the rule would still have to decide on which of the conjuncts to select in deciding what to do. This is not a matter of interpreting the rule-formulation. Where there is an agreement in practice it is perfectly clear what the expressions in the rule-formulation mean and, hence, what the rule is. The kind of judgement involved is not related to interpretation.

It was suggested that two people might end up doing different things. Someone who is reporting goodwill may be doing something different than someone reporting property, plant and equipment. In another sense, though, they are doing the same thing, for they are all reporting assets. What this shows is that doing the same thing or doing something different depends upon how what is done is described. Wittgenstein once said that 'the use of the word "rule" and the use of the word "same" are interwoven' (Wittgenstein, 1953, §225). Given that an explanation of the meaning of an expression gives a rule for its use (Baker and Hacker, 1980, p. 36), if the rule for the meaning of an expression allows it to be applied in two sets of circumstances then the circumstances *are the same*. If two things are the same this *means* the same expression applied to both. Two things can be the same and different if the same expression and different expressions are applied to them as in these examples. This makes it more difficult to understand the demand for 'consistency' in financial reporting—that is, 'the use of the same accounting policies and procedures' (FASB/IASB, 2006, QC35). In these examples those who follow the rule are using the same procedures, all reporting assets or playing a game, but are also undertaking different procedures. Are they consistent, and are the results of what they do 'comparable'?

Judgement has to be used where expressions have explanations of this kind. However, this is not because the expression is vague. It is because the explanation is of a certain kind that requires decisions or choices to be made. Standard setters may wish to avoid using expressions with explanations of this kind in order to avoid the need to exercise judgement of this kind. The predilection for expressions that have definitions in terms of necessary and sufficient conditions in accounting standards is not to avoid vagueness but rather to avoid the need to exercise a certain kind of judgement in following the rule in a standard. Definitions of this kind are not necessary to avoid vagueness. This depends only on agreement in the practice of using expressions—that is, to avoid *actual* disagreements in judgements about its applicability (Baker and Hacker, 1980, p. 218). As long as, in what might be dubbed 'normal' circumstances, there is agreement in use, expressions are not vague. As Wittgenstein puts it, 'the sign-post is in order—if, under normal circumstances, it fulfils its purpose' (Wittgenstein, 1953, §87). Expressions that are explained in other ways may have an agreed practice. There may still be agreement on their use in such 'normal' circumstances. If there are disagreements in the actual practice of using expressions in the rule-formulation then, as noted earlier, these might be overcome by the standard setters explaining what they mean by the expression in the implementation guidance included in standards. If the 'sign-post' is not in order it can be made so by implementation guidance. An explanation of the meaning of expressions is adequate provided it averts misunderstandings and 'provided it establishes an agreed pattern of application given prevailing circumstances' (Baker and Hacker, 1980, pp. 224–225).

The view that all language is vague has been called a 'caricature' of the ideas in Wittgenstein's later work and 'radically misconceived' (Baker and Hacker, 1980, pp. 215–217). What Wittgenstein actually argued was that explanations do not need to remove 'every possible doubt about how to apply an expression' (Baker and Hacker, 1980, p. 225). If this was the objective of explanation then it would be an attempt to eliminate not only actual vagueness but also *possible* vagueness. This is the objective of attaining 'determinacy of sense'.

'DETERMINACY OF SENSE'

The ideal of 'determinacy of sense' is an ideal that 'the explanation of any concept-word . . . alone determines for every object whether or not this object falls under the concept' (Baker and Hacker, 1980, p. 210). Definitions that result in 'determinacy of sense' are those that are 'complete' in the sense that they 'determine once and for all every possible application of the defined expression' and that grasping them 'will provide someone with a complete knowledge of how to use the expression' (Baker and Hacker, 1980, p. 12). They are supposed to remove *every possible doubt* about how to apply the defined expression correctly. It is sometimes assumed that definitions of an expression that set out necessary and sufficient conditions for its use achieve 'determinacy of sense', for they will provide 'complete knowledge of how to use the expression' (Baker and Hacker, 1980, p. 12). It is this objective that lies behind the 'perfect' language beloved of some philosophers. Such 'a precise formal language' is supposed to operate like a 'calculus' whereby 'from the explanation of its terms and of its structure we will be able systematically to calculate the meanings of its sentences. Indeed, these calculations might even take the form of formal derivations within an axiomatic system' (Baker and Hacker, 1980, p. 219). This is the kind of language that the FEE suggests, in the aforementioned quotation, might operate like an algorithm. There is no need for judgement in following the rule because what is in accord with the rule in all circumstances can be *deduced* from a rule that includes expressions that have a determinate sense. It is no coincidence that the demand for 'determinacy of sense' goes hand in hand with the demand for definitions in terms of necessary and sufficient conditions (Baker and Hacker, 1980, p. 220). They are thought to eliminate 'the *possibility* of vagueness' (Baker and Hacker, 1980, p. 20). In the context of accounting standards this means that the possibility of disagreeing about what the rule means—that is, what is in accord with the rule—is eliminated, for if the premises in a deduction are accepted then the conclusion follows *necessarily*. The opposite of this is 'indeterminacy of sense'—that is, the '*possibility* of vagueness' (Baker and Hacker, 1980, p. 218). This is the possibility that those who use the expressions may disagree on the practice of using them.

The ideal of a language with determinacy of sense is not only a philosopher's 'pipe-dream' (Baker and Hacker, 1980, p. 37). It is also a vision the SEC identifies as 'underlying a rules-based approach' that includes a dream to 'specify the appropriate accounting treatment for virtually every imaginable scenario, such that the determination of the appropriate accounting answer for any situation is straight-forward and, at least in theory, the extent of professional judgement is minimized' (SEC, 2003, p. 13). If the expressions used in an accounting standard do not use expressions that have 'determinacy of sense' then the standard setter might seek to achieve this result by defining the expressions by setting out necessary and sufficient conditions in implementation guidance. The 'rules-based approach' has 'an intent to minimize (and in certain instances to trivialize) the judgmental component of accounting practice through the establishment of complicated, finely articulated rules that attempt to foresee all possible application challenges' (SEC, 2003, p. 15). This results in voluminous implementation guidance where this is necessary to eliminate 'indeterminacy of sense'—that is, possible disagreements about what is in accord with the rule.

ICAS note the view that 'the rules-based approach developed in the US results from a history of rigorous and aggressive regulation of financial reporting' which was driven by 'a desire for comparability'. They suggest that 'the more comparability required, the more rules have to be put in place to enforce it' (ICAS, 2006, p. 5). In consequence there was a demand for 'uniform accounting standards which would limit management's use of professional judgment and enhance the comparability of financial statements' (Wüstemann and Wüstemann, 2010, p. 2). Further pressure for 'rules-based' standards comes from the fact that there is 'the demand of major constituents, particularly management and auditors, who want a clear answer to each and every perceivable accounting issue. The litigious situation in the United States . . . means that the risk of law suits based on alleged wrong accounting is high and gives accountants a strong incentive to ask for rules they can adhere to in a case of a costly law suit' (Benston, Bromwich and Wagenhofer, 2006, p. 168). In other words, they want rules that have 'determinacy of sense'. The threat of litigation has resulted in audit firms looking to the standard setters 'for 'bright-line' rules that could support audit opinions' (ICAS, 2006, p. 5). It is assumed that rules of this kind contain numbers and have determinacy of sense. Newton appears to have thought that language was 'a process, an act of transposition or translation—the conversion of reality into symbolic form' and that mathematics was 'symbolic translation at its purest' (Gleick, 2003, p. 36). Thus, 'he believed in mathematics as the road to understanding', for it was 'certain' (Gleick, 2003, p. 86). It is no accident that the FEE uses a mathematical term, 'algorithm', to describe a certain kind of rule. If there are no possible disagreements about the meaning of numbers there is no possibility of vagueness. It may be for this reason that the use of numbers in rules that contain 'bright-line tests' has been favoured by some standard setters, notably in the U.S. (SEC, 2003, p. 11). The demand for such standards arises out of a demand for 'determinacy of sense'. It is this demand that constituted the target for Wittgenstein's arguments.

Wittgenstein maintained that no explanation, even one that gives necessary and sufficient conditions, can provide a '*complete* explanation of meaning', one that would 'in principle remove *every possible* doubt about how to apply the defined expression correctly' (Baker and Hacker, 1980, p. 225). Wittgenstein has a nice image of how this kind of language is meant to work. A rule is seen as 'a section of rails invisibly laid to infinity', and 'infinitely long rails correspond to the unlimited application of a rule' (Wittgenstein, 1953, §218). Wittgenstein counters this image by arguing that *any* explanation of an expression that is given in words including explanations in terms of necessary and sufficient conditions might be understood differently. This is because explanations of expressions are given *in language*, and further explanations might be required of expressions used in these explanations. The same problem would arise, and this, in turn, would foster a demand for further explanation, which could also be interpreted differently by someone else. Wittgenstein asks, 'But then how does an explanation help me to understand, if after all it is not the final one? In that case the explanation is never completed; so I still don't understand what he means, and never shall!' It is 'as though an explanation as it were hung in the air unless supported by another one' (Wittgenstein, 1953, §87). The attempt to provide the further explanations thought to be necessary to eliminate indeterminacy would account for the voluminous implementation guidance in 'rules-based standards'. That 'determinacy of sense' is an unattainable ideal is implied by the SEC's statement that despite the attempts of a 'rules-based' system to minimize the exercise of judgement by accountants 'it is simply impossible to fully eliminate professional judgment in the application of accounting standards' (SEC, 2003, p. 16). Although they do not refer to the ideal as a demand for 'determinacy of sense' their observations amount to a rejection of this demand.

It can now be appreciated that Brown, Collins and Thornton's claim that Wittgenstein said all language is vague is mistaken. What Wittgenstein actually maintained was that all language has 'indeterminacy of sense'. The difference is that if language is vague there are *actual* disagreements in the practice of using the expressions. This may not be the case with much of our language and, in particular, for the language used in accounting standards. The 'sign-posts' may well be in order, at least in the 'normal' circumstances within which an expression is used and a rule applied. There may be no significant differences in the actual practice of using expressions. Implementation guidance can deal with any differences in actual practice and can assist in forging an agreed practice that eliminates vagueness or actual disagreement in practice. This does not mean there might not be *possible* disagreements in the practice of using these expressions.

Implementation guidance cannot deal with *all possible differences*. This is because it is not possible to envisage *all* the potential circumstances in which an expression may be used outside of 'normal' circumstances. This is well known in the standard setting context. Rules in accounting standards may be applied in new situations, and there may be disagreements on whether and how a rule is to be applied in such circumstances. This is precisely the worry of standard setters in the area of financial reporting when they see accountants indulging in 'financial engineering' in order to 'engineer their way around the intent of the standards' (SEC, 2003, p. 13). 'New' circumstances are created where there is no practice in following the rule, and this creates a problem because it is not clear whether a rule is to apply in such circumstances. Note that such an approach is only necessary where there is no agreed practice. It is only in areas like derivatives where there is no agreed practice that either the standard setter or the practitioner must decide. It is not surprising that this kind of problem arises in new accounting areas like derivatives. New kinds of derivatives are created, and the problem is to determine how the rules in the standards are to apply to them. There is no practice in applying rules for assets or equity to such instruments, and so some *decision* has to be made about the application of rules to them. The standard setter may attempt to deal with the problem by trying to explain how the rule is to be interpreted in possible circumstances in the implementation guidance. This approach may account for the 'detailed implementation guidance' such as the '800 pages of guidance on accounting for derivatives' included in a standard characterized as 'rules-based' (SEC, 2003, p. 23). If Wittgenstein is right that all possible circumstances in which the rule might apply cannot be envisaged then no amount of implementation guidance can achieve the ideal of determinacy of sense.

This does not mean implementation guidance is unimportant and ineffective. It is not necessary in areas where rule-formulations are not vague. However, it can deal with *actual* vagueness and assist in the application of an expression in 'normal contexts'. It can avert misunderstandings in applying the rule. However, the aim of such guidance is to deal with *actual* vagueness and not with *possible* vagueness. It does not have to try to eliminate 'indeterminacy of sense'. Standard setters should be clear about the objectives of implementation guidance. Even if the attempt to deal with possible vagueness is doomed to failure it would appear useful to include guidance where there is actual vagueness in the use of expressions. A more difficult decision would be whether or not to try and deal with what might be called *probable* vagueness. This would arise where disagreements on the use of expressions are *likely* to ensue in certain circumstances, even if, at the moment, the rule is not applied in such circumstances and, hence, there are no actual disagreements in applying the rule. If it was thought likely that rules would need to be applied in circumstances outside 'normal contexts' then it may be worthwhile to consider including implementation guidance in a standard to deal with 'probable' vagueness. Thus, implementation guidance can be used to achieve different objectives. It can be used to *educate* preparers in the actual practice of using an expression and, hence, in the actual practice of following a rule. It can be used to avert actual vagueness. It can be used to eliminate probable vagueness. It can also be used to try to avert indeterminacy of sense, although this does not seem possible.

Standard setters need to decide on the objectives of such guidance. This determines whether they decide to include such guidance in standards and, if so, how much to include. This determines the kind of standard they promulgate.

IMPLEMENTATION GUIDANCE AND KINDS OF ACCOUNTING STANDARDS

Standard setters need to decide how they will deal with any vagueness in the language used in accounting standards. If there is little or no actual vagueness in the expressions in the rule-formulation then little or no implementation guidance would be required to eliminate such vagueness. Standard setters might have the objective of formulating standards using only language that is not vague, for then they would not need to include any or much implementation guidance that has, as its goal, the elimination of vagueness. If there is actual vagueness in the language used in an accounting standard then standard setters can include implementation guidance to eliminate it by setting out the meaning of expressions in the rule-formulation. They can use their 'collective judgement' to determine what the expressions are to mean and, thus, how the standard is to be interpreted. How much guidance is needed depends on the extent of actual vagueness. More will be appropriate where there is considerable vagueness and less where most expressions are not vague and there is an agreed practice in using these expressions.

Even if there is actual vagueness the standard setter may decide not to include implementation guidance but rather leave it to the preparer to interpret the rule-formulation. In effect, instead of applying the 'collective judgement' of the standard setter the exercise of judgement in interpreting the expressions in the rule-formulation—that is, in determining what the rule is *to be*—can be left to those who follow the rule. They should be guided, as the standard setter is guided, by a grasp of the objectives of the standard, perhaps derived from the conceptual framework, in exercising this judgement. These objectives may be stated in the accounting standard so that those who follow the rule are made aware of these objectives. They are constrained by the same conventions that prevent the standard setter from determining any meaning they like for certain expressions. If it is left to those who follow the rules to exercise their judgement in the face of vague expressions then it will not be appropriate to include guidance in the standard to resolve this vagueness.

Where it is left to the rule followers to exercise judgement in determining what the rule is to mean, it is possible they will use this discretion to overcome the problem that may arise with accounting standards that following a rule may not always meet the objectives of the rule in all circumstances where it could be applied. What might happen in such circumstances is that the rule is 'interpreted' to exclude these circumstances from the ambit of the rule. This problem can also be addressed by standard setters through the use of exceptions in a standard or allowing an override in such circumstances where the reporting system allows it to be used. Leaving the interpretation of the rule to the rule follower has dangers, for the interpretation may be seen as purely instrumental in avoiding an inconvenient consequence of following a rule and may override or stretch any existing conventions that may constrain interpretation. Different rule followers may arrive at different decisions depending on how far they are willing to go in bending meanings to this end.

If any of these strategies are adopted by standard setters in setting accounting standards it is possible to argue that the amount of guidance included in standards is *appropriate*. If language is not vague it is appropriate to include little or no guidance. If the standard setter wishes to eliminate actual vagueness then she will include sufficient guidance to ensure that the practice of using the expressions in the rule-formulations is agreed. If the standard setter wishes to leave the interpretation of standards to the rule follower then it is appropriate not to include guidance in the standard. In all circumstances it could be agreed that the appropriate amount of guidance is included in the accounting standard. Agreement about this masks considerable possible disagreement about whether or not expressions are vague and whether to exercise collective judgement or to allow rule followers to exercise judgement in interpreting standards. A further issue that should be considered is whether standard setters should have as an objective the elimination of probable vagueness. This will have implications for how much guidance is appropriate if it is to be provided in accounting standards.

Standard setters may not be content to deal only with actual vagueness. They may also want to eliminate possible vagueness—that is, wish to achieve determinacy of sense. As suggested earlier this may require the inclusion of voluminous implementation guidance in the standard as this may be appropriate in the attempt to achieve this end. It was suggested that having such an objective is actually inappropriate given that determinacy of sense is not an achievable ideal. This means that including implementation guidance to achieve an inappropriate ideal is itself inappropriate. What is inappropriate is having such an objective in the first place. If this is the objective of 'rules-based' standards then it can be argued that the amount of guidance included in such standards is inappropriate. If a contrast is suggested between 'rules-based' standards and 'principles-based' standards then it might be argued that the latter but not the former contain an 'appropriate amount of implementation guidance'. This is one of the criteria of 'principles-based' standards identified by the SEC (SEC, 2003, p. 12). If the reason for including inappropriate amounts of guidance is that the wrong objective—that is, eliminating indeterminacy of sense—is adopted then the contrast between 'principles-based' and 'rules-based' standards should really be a contrast between standards devised with the objective of eliminating indeterminacy of sense and those without such an objective. Standards without such an objective may be 'principles-based' and may include an appropriate amount of guidance but can be very different because they mask disagreement about whether or not expressions are vague and whether to exercise collective judgement or to allow rule followers to exercise judgement in interpreting standards.

It is suggested here that if progress is to be made in identifying a target kind of standard for standard setters then some discussion should take place as to the importance of identifying if the language used in accounting standards is vague, what this means and how it can be overcome. There should also be agreement on the means of overcoming this problem. Standard setters need to agree on whether they should exercise collective judgement in determining the meaning of these expressions and should include sufficient implementation guidance to eliminate different interpretations of the standard or if they should leave the judgement about meanings to the individual judgement of those who follow the standard. There can be agreement on the need to promulgate 'principles-based' standards, understood as those standards that include an 'appropriate amount of implementation guidance', without agreement about these other important issues. The use of the expression 'principles-based' understood in this way masks these issues and fosters the appearance of agreement when there may be no underlying agreement about the nature of accounting standards.

This chapter has focused on problems that arise in following standards that are vague and on the use of implementation guidance as an attempt to overcome vagueness, understood in various ways—that is, actual, probable or possible vagueness. There may be another 'problem' with language that standard setters need to confront. Implementation guidance can also be used where the meaning of the expressions used in the rule-formulation are not vague but do involve alternatives.

ANOTHER USE OF IMPLEMENTATION GUIDANCE

Differences in following rules can arise if the rule uses an expression explained by setting out alternatives. One example of this would be an explanation by enumeration where the meaning of an expression is given by enumerating the things that come under the expression. Thus 'day of the week' may be explained by enumeration such as 'a day of the week is either Monday or Tuesday or Wednesday . . . ' If someone is commanded to 'go and see your mother on a day of the week' then it is clear he must go and see his mother on either Monday or Tuesday or Wednesday. . . . Clearly, someone giving the command who grasps this meaning does not care whether the person commanded goes on Monday or Tuesday or Wednesday. . . . Someone commanded to see his mother on a day of the week has to decide which day to go. The interesting thing is that someone can fulfil the command by going to see his mother on Wednesday. He does not *deduce* the desire to see his mother on Wednesday from a desire to do what is commanded and a grasp of the meaning of 'day of the week'. Some judgement needs to be exercised—that is, some choice or decision needs to be made—if the command is accepted.

An example of an expression from the accounting context that can be explained in this way is that of 'depreciation'. This expression might be explained by saying that depreciation involves the allocation of the cost of an asset over its useful life using a choice from among 'the straight-line method, the diminishing balance method and the units of production method' (IASB, 2013, IAS 16, §62). An accounting standard that required non-current assets to be depreciated could be followed by someone using either method. IAS 16 states that 'each part of an item of property, plant and equipment with a cost that is significant in relation to the total cost of the item shall be depreciated separately' (IASB, 2013, IAS 16, §43). Standard setters who set a standard that simply required non-current assets to be depreciated may not care which of the methods were used and would allow those who follow the standard to exercise judgement in determining what to do in following this standard. Those who follow the standard could not deduce which of the methods to use from the desire to follow a rule like this. They would have to made a decision or choice in following the rule. Implementation guidance could set out which of the methods was to be used for different kinds of non-current assets. This would obviate the necessity to exercise judgement. In effect, it substitutes more specific rules regarding depreciation of particular kinds of assets. In fact, IAS 16 allows those who follow the rule to exercise judgement but sets out factors that are to be used in exercising this judgement—that is, what considerations are to be taken into account in making decisions or choices that are required by following a rule of this kind. It states that 'the depreciation method used shall reflect the pattern in which the asset's future economic benefits are expected to be consumed by the entity' (IASB, 2013, IAS 16, §60). Implementation guidance in IAS 16 is not designed to address the problem of vagueness, for there may be no vagueness in an expression explained by enumeration.

IMPLICATIONS FOR STANDARD SETTERS

The findings in this chapter have implications for standard setters. It is important for them to be aware of the problems involved in using language in rule-formulations in accounting standards. The ideal language to use would be one where there is an agreed usage of the expressions where everyone who follows accounting standards is aware of the practice and, hence, there is agreement on what rule is expressed in the rule-formulation. Where there is some ignorance of the practice then the standard setter can address this problem by including implementation guidance in the standard that has an educational role in informing those who follow standards about the meaning of the expressions in the rule-formulation. If there are a number of different practices in the use of expressions—that is, where the rule is vague and there is no agreed practice in their use—then standard setters can use implementation guidance to indicate their preferred practice and, hence, to indicate how they mean the rule-formulation to be interpreted. 'Interpretation', here, is understood as giving a meaning to expressions in rule-formulations. Where there are few or no agreed practices in the use of expressions then the standard setter can use implementation guidance to determine what the practice is to be and, hence, what rule is expressed by the rule-formulation. The chapter suggests that implementation guidance can be aimed at addressing actual vagueness, where there are actual differences in using expressions, or probable vagueness, where although there may be no disagreement in practice at the moment it is likely the rule will be applied in circumstances where it is likely there will be disagreements. Implementation guidance should not be used to deal with possible vagueness—that is, where there is no actual or probable disagreement in the use of expressions in rule-formulations but where there is the possibility of disagreement if the rule is followed in circumstances where it is not applied or is applied in unknown circumstances. Attempting to deal with such vagueness is to aim for determinacy of sense, which is an impossible ideal.

Although the standard setter can opt to deal with vagueness in one or another of its forms through the inclusion of implementation guidance in standards, another possibility is to leave it to those who follow such standards to deal with vagueness. In other words, the judgement in determining the meaning of expressions in rule-formulations where they are vague is not exercised by the standard setter but rather is left to those who follow accounting standards. If this option is chosen then it becomes important to ensure that those who follow standards are aware of the objectives of the standard—that is, what desires the standard is meant to achieve. It was suggested that if agreement on these objectives is to be reached so that those who follow standards interpret them in the same way then it would be useful to include these objectives or desires in the standards themselves. This thought lies behind one of the characteristics that 'principles-based' standards are supposed to exemplify—that is, such standards should include a statement of the objectives of the standard.

It is clear from these findings that standard setters need to make choices about the content and objectives of implementation guidance and the strategy for dealing with vagueness in language. Although a number of pronouncements by standard setters, particularly those that arise out of the debate over 'principles-based' versus 'rules-based' standards, suggest involvement with the issue of such choices, they have not been tackled systematically. The use of these terms to identify different kinds of standards obscures some of the real issues and prevents a proper debate about certain important issues in standard setting. Some of the tools available in the philosophy of language have not been used in thinking about these issues. This chapter provides the requisite perspective for examining and resolving these issues. The conclusion is that judgement is not always required in interpreting the requirements of accounting standards. It is only required where there is no agreed practice in using expressions in rule-formulations. Where it is required, the judgement in determining the meaning of expressions in the rule-formulations can be exercised either by those who follow the rules in the standards or by standard setters. Standard setters need to decide where, and to what extent, they will deal with vagueness or leave it to those who follow the standards. This decision will, in turn, determine the objectives of implementation guidance and the amount of such guidance required. If standard setters do not wish to allow judgement in interpreting rules then they must include sufficient implementation guidance to eliminate ambiguity. If the objective is to eliminate all ambiguity (i.e. determinacy of sense) then there will be a need for, possibly endless, implementation guidance. Even so it is unlikely it can be eliminated. This decision determines the extent of judgement to be exercised by preparers of financial statements in interpreting accounting standards. Disallowing judgement results in no effective way of dealing with ambiguity.

SUMMARY

This chapter has examined the use of judgement in interpreting accounting standards. Judgement of this kind is necessary whenever the language used in rule-formulations is vague. Language is vague whenever there is *no agreed practice* in the use of expressions in the rule-formulation. One way in which such vagueness can be overcome is by standard setters exercising collective judgement in deciding how the standard is to be interpreted and then indicating this by including implementation guidance in the standard. The argument that all language is vague and thus that all rule-formulations need to be interpreted is considered and rejected. The argument that all language is vague is sometimes confused with the argument that all language lacks 'determinacy of sense'. This is the idea that understanding language implies that *every possible doubt* about how to apply an expression correctly is removed. The attempt to realize this ideal leads to the demand for voluminous implementation guidance to eliminate 'indeterminacy of sense'—that is, all possible disagreements about what is in accord with the rule. Wittgenstein's argument that all such doubts cannot be eliminated is examined. Although implementation guidance may eliminate actual or probable vagueness it is not possible to formulate guidance that will eliminate possible vagueness. It is suggested that standard setters must get clear about the objective of including implementation guidance in standards and whether it is there to try and eliminate actual, probable or possible vagueness. It is suggested that an alternative to standard setters attempting to eliminate vagueness in rule-formulations is to leave it to those who follow standards to interpret the rule-formulations themselves. This allows judgement in determining what the rule is, given the rule-formulation, to be left to those who follow the standards rather than to the standard setter. If this is to be done then it is important for those who follow the standards to be aware of the objectives of the standard so this may guide their exercise of judgement.

6 The Nature and Role of Objectives in Accounting Standards

In the previous two chapters two different reasons for including objectives in accounting standards were identified. It is useful to include objectives in standards where there is a rule in the standard that is understood as a 'rule of thumb' where the rule can be overridden if following it on a particular occasion will not meet the objectives which prompted the promulgation of the rule in the first place. If standard setters conceive of a rule in this way then those who follow it need to be aware of the objectives of the rule if they are to exercise their judgement in deciding to override the rule on particular occasions. It was also suggested that a grasp of objectives is required where the rule-formulation includes expressions that are, in some sense, vague so that those who follow the rule are able to 'interpret' the rule. This amounts to determining what the rule expressed by the rule-formulation actually is. In reasoning to this interpretation a grasp of objectives is necessary in precisely the way it is necessary when standard setters promulgate the rule in the first place. In effect, those following the rule are determining what the rule *is to be*. Interpreting a rule is simply promulgating a rule to be followed. The objectives of the rule are used in adjudicating between possible interpretations of the rule given that not anything counts as an interpretation of a rule-formulation.

Both these justifications for the inclusion of objectives in accounting standards show that the objectives perform the same kind of function as the objectives included in conceptual frameworks that assist the standard setter in promulgating standards. The decision to promulgate a standard involves reasoning from a desire to bring about a certain end to a desire to adopt a rule believed to bring about the end. The action of following a rule is also guided by such desires. If following the rule on a particular occasion will not achieve the objectives then it is not to be followed. Interpreting a rule-formulation is a matter of considering what interpretation—that is, what rule given the rule-formulation—will achieve the objectives standard setters have in mind in promulgating the rule. The reasoning required in making decisions about the override of rules or interpreting rule-formulations is similar to that involved in promulgating standards. It was suggested in chapter 3 that this reasoning was nondeductive practical reasoning. If either of these two exercises of judgement are allowed to those who follow accounting standards then similar reasoning to these decisions will need to take place. Ensuring that those who make these decisions in following standards are aware of the objectives of the rule makes it sensible to include a statement of the objectives in the standard. It might be surmised that because standards that are 'principles-based' allow those who follow rules to exercise judgement of this kind then it makes sense to define this kind of standard, as the SEC do, as one that 'involves a concise statement of substantive accounting principle where the accounting objective has been incorporated as an integral part of the standard' (SEC, 2003, p. 12). The problem with this reason for including objectives is that it is not clear whether standards that are claimed to be 'principles-based' actually need to include objectives to be used for such a purpose. Not everyone who supports the idea of 'principles-based' standards appears to allow the exercises of judgement that the objectives might be thought to underpin. Some standards that include objectives do not include the kinds of expressions of desires that are to be used in reasoning to these kind of decisions. In order to see this, the idea of 'principles-based' standards will be examined in a conceptual enquiry into this concept. A similar enquiry will be made into the idea of an objective as understood by standard setters who include objectives in standards.

A CONCEPTUAL ENQUIRY INTO 'PRINCIPLES-BASED' STANDARDS

One influential explanation of the 'principles-based' approach to standard setting is provided by the report of the Principles versus Rules Working Group set up by ICAS. It states that 'principles-based' accounting standards are based on a conceptual framework (ICAS, 2006, p. 1). They go on to say that such standards 'require a clear hierarchy of overarching concepts, principles that reflect the overarching concepts and limited further guidance' (ICAS, 2006, p. 7). They define a principle as 'a general statement, with widespread support, which is intended to support truth and fairness and acts as a guide to action.' They maintain that 'principles cannot be replaced by mechanical rules' (ICAS, 2006, p. 4). This explanation of the nature of 'principles-based' standards is deficient in a number of ways. The characteristics meant to identify such standards flow seamlessly between those that identify standards that are 'based on principles' and standards that express 'principles'. Standards 'based on' principles in a conceptual framework are principles-based, but the idea that principles guide action and contrast with mechanical rules suggests that principles-based standards are those that contain prescriptions of a certain kind that are distinguished from rules. The ICAS ignores the difference between these two senses of 'principles-based' and hurries on to the question of the characteristics of the prescriptions that appear in accounting standards and the contrast between the two kinds of prescription which are called, respectively, 'rules' and 'principles'. Most of the study relates to a discussion of the relative merits of these two kinds of prescriptions rather than the merits of standards based on principles in a conceptual framework. Although evidence is provided for the support that exists for principles-based accounting there is little detailed exploration of what the interviewees actually mean by the word 'principle' and what it is for a standard to be principles-based. This undermines the message derived from the interviews. It is not clear exactly what the interviewees had in mind in giving support for principles-based standards.

The lack of clarity in the explanation derives from a failure to grasp that there are two distinct concepts of being 'principles-based' (Dennis, 2008, p. 265). One concept identifies standards which are derived by a standard setting process that starts by considering 'principles' expressed in a conceptual framework. The exact nature of principles in a conceptual framework is problematic. In particular, it is not clear whether such principles are meant to express what is wanted from financial reporting, something along the lines of the objectives statement supplemented by the chapter on qualitative characteristics, or whether they are meant to express some kind of prescription, perhaps of a general kind that allows the derivation of other more specific prescriptions which are included in accounting standards. This distinction was examined in chapter 3. This raises important issues of the precise logical nature of the statements in a conceptual framework as well as what kind of reasoning is to be used by standard setters in deriving standards from the principles in the framework. These issues are largely ignored in the literature on conceptual frameworks. Despite the problems in understanding the nature of principles and what it means for standards to be 'based on' them there is considerable support for the idea that standards should be based on principles. The alternative of promulgating 'ad hoc' standards or standards 'based on' the political interests of various lobbying groups is not attractive. Most would agree that *any* reasonable accounting standard should, in some sense, have this characteristic. This suggests that being 'based on' a conceptual framework is not a characteristic that differentiates one kind of standard from another in any other sense than that it differentiates 'ad hoc' from reasoned standards (Dennis, 2008, p. 265).

The lack of clarity in the explanations of what it is for a standard to be principles-based is not surprising given the failure to get clear about the nature of principles of accounting as evidenced in the history of the search for 'principles' in the twentieth century. It was suggested in chapter 3 that the idea of a 'principle' of accounting, as it is understood as the kind of thing included in one kind of 'theory' of accounting, is ambiguous as between general rules or conventions and the ends or objectives—that is, general desires that are to be achieved by the promulgation of standards—of the kind included in conceptual frameworks. It is no wonder that little help was derived from looking back at the 'principles and postulates' debate of the 1960s and 1970s (ICAS, 2006, p. 4). The ICAS should have learned the lesson of history and avoided entanglement with 'principles'. Their own definition is so vague that the nature of 'principles' is scarcely indicated. It does not explain what kind of 'general statement' a 'principle' is supposed to be. It could mean a *general prescription* of what is to be done or else a *general desire* to be fulfilled all or most of the time. The fact that a 'principle' is a 'guide to action' does not distinguish the sense in which prescriptions guide actions by setting out what must be done from the sense in which desires guide actions through practical or instrumental reasoning from what is wanted and what action is believed to fulfil this desire to a desire to act. It is unclear how prescriptions 'support truth and fairness'. Does this mean that by following the prescriptions, doing what is required, truth and fairness in financial reporting results? Are the 'principles' supposed to guide the standard setter in *producing* prescriptions that, if followed, result in true and fair financial reporting?

A similar equivocation is evident elsewhere in the literature. In Alexander's description of different types of criteria used in approaches to determining the adequacy of financial statements it is not clear whether 'Type A' criteria—that is, 'a generally expressed all-pervasive fundamental concept' (Alexander, 1999, p. 240)—are prescriptions or desires. Nobes equates these, and also 'Type B' criteria—that is, 'a set of rules, conventions or ways of thinking which are to be consistently applied to situations both familiar or unfamiliar' (Alexander, 1999, p. 240)—with 'principles' (Nobes, 2005, p. 26). This is mysterious since 'concepts' would appear to be a rather different thing from 'rules' or 'conventions'. The FASB calls the chapters in their conceptual framework 'statements of financial accounting concepts' (SFACs). The UK Accounting Standards Board calls their conceptual framework a 'statement of principles'. Both are unclear as to what kind of thing their statements *state*. Are they desires or prescriptions?

Standards can be 'principles-based' in that they are 'based on principles' but still not be 'principles-based' in that they do not contain prescriptions that have the qualities that define such standards as principles-based (Schipper, 2003, p. 62). The characteristics that differentiate prescriptions in standards between 'rules' and 'principles' are implied by some of the characteristics set out in the SEC study. A 'principles-based' standard is one that has these characteristics:

  i) includes few, if any, 'exceptions or internal inconsistencies'
  ii) provides an 'appropriate amount of implementation guidance'
  iii) is devoid of 'bright-line tests' (SEC, 2003, p. 12)

To these characteristics might be added another that is identified by ICAS, namely that 'principles-based' standards should do the following:

  iv) allow for the exercise of judgement (ICAS, 2006, p.1)

This final characteristic has support elsewhere (Schipper, 2003, p. 61; FASB, 2002).

There are a number of problems in understanding these characteristics and applying them in determining whether or not a standard is principles-based. There are some obvious questions about how they are to be understood. What is meant by the words 'few' or 'appropriate' in the expression of the characteristics? There can be different views about whether a standard includes few exceptions or an appropriate amount of implementation guidance. This may result in different judgements about whether or not a standard is principles-based. It is not clear whether *all* these characteristics have to be present if a standard is to be said to be 'principles-based' (Dennis, 2008, p. 266). The SEC recognises that some standards might be called 'principles-based' even if they do not have *all* the characteristics of being 'principles-based'. These characteristics are thus not *necessary* conditions for a standard to be 'principles-based'. The SEC refer to this concept as an 'ideal variant', which means that standards of this kind may have *most* but not all of the characteristics. They recognise that standards may only 'approach' the ideal (SEC, 2003, p. 24). It has been suggested that the concepts of being 'principles-based' and 'rules-based' form 'a continuum' (AAA, 2003, p. 74). A similar problem exists in the area of law. These concepts have been described as 'crude' (Cunningham, 2007, p. 1413) and 'imperfect' (Cunningham, 2007, p. 1492). It is suggested that 'accounting systems, like corporate law and securities regulation, defy tidy classification as rules-based or principles-based' (Cunningham, 2007, p. 1460). Given that these characteristics are not necessary conditions, standards can be called 'principles-based' if they have only *some* of the characteristics. The perception of the relative importance of these characteristics may vary. Standards that are 'principles-based' can have different collections of such characteristics, and groups of standard setters and professionals using this expression can have different collections in mind when they refer to a standard as 'principles-based'. There is no 'checklist' of characteristics that has to be ticked before a standard can be termed 'principles-based'.

Different perceptions about the meaning of the expressions that describe these characteristics and different practices in deciding how many and which of the characteristics need to be present for a standard to be principles-based may result in differences in the use of the expression amongst different people. The term is vague. This does not necessarily mean the concept is not useful for some purposes. The characteristics identified by the SEC for 'principles-based' standards may be 'a sensible and desirable list of characteristics and admonitions' that amounts to something of a 'wish list' (Benston, Bromwich and Wagenhofer, 2006, p. 170). No standard has to have all these characteristics to count as 'principles-based', but different people may have a different 'wish list' in mind when they consider whether or not a standard is 'principles-based'. This is important given the attempt to achieve convergence of accounting standards. A particular standard with a particular set of characteristics may be acceptable to one party and not to another.

The potential disagreements about whether or not a standard is 'principles-based' are revealed by different explanations and/or by the failure to agree on whether or not a standard is of this kind. What is not so obvious is that these disagreements in meaning may result from underlying differences in either what is wanted in the ideal accounting standard or in beliefs as to what kind of standard will achieve what is wanted. In particular, there may be differences in perceptions as to how some of the problems of standard setting are to be dealt with. The problems these characteristics are meant to assist in dealing with are those set out in chapters 4 and 5. Restricting the number of exceptions in standards makes sense if the problems of promulgating standards that, if followed, do not always meet the objectives that prompt their adoption are to be dealt with by the exercise of judgement in overriding the standard on such occasions. Restricting the amount of implementation guidance needed in standards makes sense where the language used in rule-formulations in the standard is ambiguous, and this is to be dealt with by the exercise of judgement in interpreting the rule-formulations. In both cases the exercise of judgement is required and the inclusion of objectives is useful to guide such judgement. This provides a justification for including the characteristic that 'principles-based' standards include a statement of the objective of the standard as indicated in the SEC study as well as the importance of the exercise of judgement in such standards highlighted by ICAS. To what extent do standards that are 'principles-based' actually incorporate a statement of objectives in this sense, though?

OBJECTIVES IN STANDARDS

In chapter 3 the idea of an objective was explained as something expressed as the first premise in practical reasoning to the action of standard setting. The standard setter wants to achieve some end by performing the intentional action of setting standards and then considers beliefs about what rules will achieve these ends in order to conclude with a desire to promulgate a rule. An objective is an expression of what is wanted from the action of setting standards. Another way of explaining a 'principles-based' standard is that it is a standard promulgated by reasoning from a premise of this kind. Such premises are expressed in conceptual frameworks. This explains the idea of a 'principles-based' standard as a standard 'based on' a conceptual framework. As the SEC explain, another characteristic of such standards is that they are 'consistent with, and derived from, a coherent conceptual framework' (SEC, 2003, p. 12). Including a statement of the objectives of a standard in an accounting standard itself, in this sense, would inform those who follow the standard about the reasons for its promulgation—that is, it sets out premises that would appear in practical reasoning to the desire to promulgate a standard.

Including objectives in a standard may be important in establishing the legitimacy of the standard setter in that it might be used to prove the standard setter promulgates standards for 'good' reasons. That the statements in a conceptual framework may be used in this way has been observed a number of times. Archer suggests there may have been more than one objective in constructing a conceptual framework. He says it 'is not very clear exactly what the FASB was seeking, for it appeared to be pursuing two different goals: to develop a basis in accounting theory for standards of financial accounting and reporting; and to develop a kind of constitution which would provide political legitimacy for the FASB's standard-setting' (Archer, 1993, p. 70). Dopuch and Sunder also identify a similar objective in their claim that 'the FASB has . . . little defence against the criticism that it does not have legitimate authority to make decisions which affect wealth transfers among members of society' and, hence, 'a body like the FASB needs a conceptual framework to boost its public standing' (Dopuch and Sunder, 1980, p. 17). There is nothing inconsistent in these two objectives. It is quite possible that a conceptual framework is conceived as a 'theory' that sets out the objectives, or what is wanted, from financial reporting as well as something that gives legitimacy to standard setters. Actions can have more than one motivation. The reasons given allow the action to be redescribed. For example, if a framework is used it may be because those using it want a theoretical underpinning for their actions. Using the framework may be redescribed as an action of underpinning standards with theory. They may also want to give legitimacy to their standards by showing that the standards are underpinned by theory. Using the framework can also be redescribed as giving legitimacy to standards. There is no inconsistency in these two descriptions. It is, of course, possible that one of these is not a valid description of the action if the motivation was not, actually, present. In chapter 3 we explored the motivation to base standard setting decisions on a 'theory' of accounting of a particular kind. We did not explore the idea that conceptual frameworks are used to give legitimacy to standard setters. Accepting that this might be the case does not undermine their use in providing a theoretical underpinning for accounting standard setting decisions. The use of frameworks in giving legitimacy is not further explored here. In this chapter the role of theory, in particular the role of objectives in a theory, and the role of objectives in standards are further examined.

Given that objectives of the kind that appear in conceptual frameworks perform a role in decision-making in standard setting situations, it is to be expected that when the interpretation of a rule-formulation is allowed to those who follow standards then the same kinds of objectives would be used in exercising the judgement implicit in practical reasoning to decisions about interpretation. This follows from the suggestion that interpreting a rule-formulation amounts to the same kind of decision about adopting a rule that is made by standard setters in promulgating standards. One would expect that the objectives in standards would be the same kind as those that as appear in conceptual frameworks. Similarly, given that following a rule in a standard is justified by the objectives it is meant to achieve, it is reasonable to think that the same kind of objectives would also justify not following the standard and allowing an override.

In chapter 3 the idea that objectives express something always wanted to be achieved in setting standards was examined. It was argued that this kind of 'universal desire' that might be used in deductive reasoning to derive a desire to promulgate standards may not be realistic and may result in the manufacture of universal desires, such as those that involve the construction of an ideal user whose needs are always to be met, that may not be acceptable. An alternative way of conceiving a conceptual framework was suggested whereby the objectives are understood as *general* desires used in conjunction with beliefs to derive standards in accordance with *nondeductive* practical reasoning. The desires in the conceptual framework are not expressions of something *universally* wanted but rather expressions of something *generally* desired. Where this is the case judgement needs to be exercised by the standard setter in deciding between possibly conflicting general desires in specific standard setting decisions. If this is the case then stating the objectives in a standard would be useful in informing those who are to follow the standards which of the general desires motivated the promulgation of the standard. These desires might then be used in any decisions that those following the standard may need to make, for example, decisions relating to an override of the standard or in interpreting the rule-formulation in the standard. Do the objectives in 'principles-based' standards express desires of this kind, and are they the same kinds of objectives that appear in the conceptual framework?

A quick review of some of the international accounting standards of the IASB shows that this is not the case. One of the latest standards is IFRS 13, where the objective is given as 'This IFRS: (a) defines *fair value*; (b) sets out in a single IFRS a framework for measuring fair value; and (c) requires disclosures about fair value measurements' (IASB, 2013, IFRS 13). This is really a statement of what the standard is doing or, more accurately, what the standard setters are doing in promulgating the standard. It might be a useful 'table of contents' to inform the reader of what to expect in the standard, but it does not given any reasons for promulgating the standard as it is—that is, any objectives or desires that are to be achieved by the standard. It does not set out objectives in the sense in which they are understood in conceptual frameworks. They do not express reasons of the kind that would appear in practical reasoning to the desire to perform an action or to explain why an action was performed. They would not be the kind of thing that could be used by those who follow the standard to decide whether or not to override the standard. It would not give any guidance to those who have to exercise judgement in interpreting the rule-formulation in the standard. As such its usefulness is rather limited. Why should the inclusion or otherwise of a 'table of contents' be a useful way of distinguishing different kinds of standards, those that are 'principles-based' or 'objectives-oriented' as opposed to standard of some other kind? Similar comments may be made about some of the other objectives in the IASB's accounting standards. IFRS 10 gives as its objective 'to establish principles for the presentation and preparation of consolidated financial statements when an entity controls one or more other entities' (IASB, 2013, IFRS 10); IAS 2 says the objective is 'to prescribe the accounting treatment for Inventories' (IASB, 2013, IAS 2); IAS 16 has its objective 'to prescribe the accounting treatment for property, plant and equipment'. Other standards have similar objectives.

'Objectives' have also been interpreted in other ways. An example from auditing standards will make this clear. ISA 500 requires the auditor to obtain sufficient appropriate audit evidence to be able to draw reasonable conclusions on which to base the auditor's opinion. Auditors must do something that makes it clear they have sufficient appropriate audit evidence. This might be called the objective of the action. Such a requirement is 'objectives-oriented'. This can be used to restate the requirement in terms of an objective. In ISA 500 the objective is stated as 'the objective of the auditor is to design and perform audit procedures in such a way as to enable the auditor to obtain sufficient appropriate audit evidence to be able to draw reasonable conclusions on which to base the auditor's opinion' (IAASB, 2010, ISA 500). This is just a restatement of the requirement to obtain sufficient appropriate audit evidence. There appears to be a fudge going on here. Objectives, at least as expressed in a conceptual framework, are things that are desired to be brought about by the actions of financial reporting. The manoeuvre of restating a requirement for action to bring about an objective enables an objective to be stated and, hence, enables standard setters to claim a standard is 'objectives-oriented'. This manoeuvre was observed at the time auditing standards were being revised as part of the Clarity Project. An objection was made during the due process of developing new auditing standards that the objectives of the standard were nothing more than requirements restated (Dennis, 2010a, p. 298). Anyone could agree that standards should state objectives in this sense in so far as they agree that standards should express requirements. Given that any standard expresses requirements, this characteristic does not distinguish one kind of standard from another. The distinction between objectives that express requirements and those that express desires can be used to understand *a* distinction between 'principles-based' and 'rules-based' standards, though not necessarily the one intended by some of those who use these terms.

SUMMARY

The previous two chapters suggest that including objectives in standards is useful where those who follow the standards have to exercise judgement in deciding whether or not to override standards or in interpreting rule-formulations in accounting standards. One characteristic of 'principles-based' standards is that they are standards that include statements of objectives. This suggests that one way of understanding 'principles-based' standards is that they are a kind of standard that includes rules that can be overridden and rules that need interpretation. A review of the idea of 'principles-based' standards lends some support for such a conception, but it is also clear that such standards may also be understood as standards based on 'principles' in a conceptual framework. It is also clear that standards that include objectives may not include the kind of thing—that is, 'principles'— that appears in conceptual frameworks, and they are not used for the kinds of decisions for which objectives in such frameworks are used. A review of objectives in the IASB's accounting standards illustrates the different use of objectives in standards from those in conceptual frameworks.

7   The Anatomy of Accounting Standards

The discussion of objectives in standards in the previous chapter demonstrates that in order to understand accounting standards it is important to understand the underlying purposes of standard setting and the assumptions that are made about regulation through setting standards. These purposes and assumptions have been identified and discussed in the preceding chapters. Grasping them should facilitate an understanding of what needs to be included in accounting standards and why.

A quick review of some of the International Accounting Standards of the IASB does not reveal a common structure for accounting standards. The reason for this is that standards are not all trying to do the same thing. Their purposes are different. IFRS 10 sets out 'principles for the presentation and preparation of consolidated financial statements', and the point of IAS 16 is to 'prescribe the accounting treatment for property, plant and equipment'. Both have the purpose of setting out prescriptions, whether they be principles or rules. This might be understood as 'requirements' that those who follow the standard must meet. This is explicitly recognised in IRFS 10 where there is a section called 'accounting requirements', but in IAS 16 there is no separate section referred to as 'requirements'. There are requirements, however, that are designated by the use of the word 'shall' and amount to requirements to measure property, plant and equipment at recognition and after recognition and to depreciate such assets. IFRS 13 does not have the purpose of requiring certain elements to be recorded at fair value, but rather has as its objective the 'definition of fair value' and setting out 'a framework for measuring fair value'. It does set out a requirement for 'disclosures about fair value measurements', but this only applies where such measurements have been made. Given the different purposes of the standards the content or anatomy of standards may be different. In what follows, the work in the previous chapters will be used to explain the content of such standards. Requirements will be examined first.

REQUIREMENTS IN STANDARDS

In chapter 2 it was suggested that the actions of accountants should be understood as actions of following rules, understood in the generic sense of prescriptions of a general kind that guide behaviour. Accountants follow a 'logic of appropriateness' where the first premise in reasoning to accounting actions expresses a desire to act in accord with a rule—that is, to adopt a practice of following a rule. In order to conclude with a desire to perform an accounting action the accountant must understand what is in accord with the rule—that is, the meaning of the expressions in the rule-formulation. It was suggested that the practice of accounting today is an institutional practice where rules are followed because they are required by an institution whose authority is accepted or it is a legal practice where the rules are followed because they are required by the law. In EU countries the legislature requires accountants to follow the rules established by an institution, the IASB. The requirements are set out in accounting standards that state the rules to be followed by accountants. Where the purpose of the standard is to establish rules then, obviously, there will be a section that sets out the rules to be followed, whether or not they come under a section of the standard labelled 'requirements'.

Accounting standards do not have to include rules that govern the behaviour of accountants. One understanding of a 'principles-only' approach would be one where the standard setter does not prescribe specific actions in particular kinds of circumstances but, rather, prescribes accountants to *do something* that will bring about an end, desire or objective without setting out what has to be done in order to achieve this result. What is being prescribed is not an action but a requirement for accountants to achieve a desired outcome. It might still be described as a 'prescription' or 'rule' in the generic sense, but it is a 'rule with a hole' to be filled in by the accountant following it. The 'rule' or 'principle' says to 'do something', not to do something specific. If standard setters prescribe standards with prescriptions or rules of this kind then they are leaving it to the judgement of accountants who follow them to undertake the reasoning from what is, in effect, the expression of a desire to the adoption of a rule requiring actions in kinds of circumstances or to individual actions believed to meet the ends required. Standards that set out these kinds of prescriptions are really telling accountants what they must want to achieve in accounting actions and not what they must do in order to achieve what is wanted. Accounting standards do not, in general, adopt this 'principles-only' approach, but generally specify specific actions to be undertaken in particular kinds of circumstances.

In chapter 3 it was argued that there are two different conceptions of rules of the kind that set out specific actions that might be expressed in an accounting standard. On one conception of rules—that is, rules on the 'practice' conception—a rule is something that has to be followed on *all* occasions when it applies and not just on those occasions where following it will meet the objectives that prompted the promulgation of the rule in the first place. The other conception of rules is to take them as 'rules of thumb'. This kind of rule is to be followed when doing so will meet the objectives of the rule, but the rule can be overridden where, on a particular occasion, following the rule will not achieve the desired ends. In chapter 4 these two conceptions of rules were used to consider the standard setter's response to the problem of accounting standards that are not believed to achieve the desires which prompt their acceptance on all occasions to which they apply. It was suggested that where the 'practice' conception of rules is adopted by a standard setter then the response to this problem is to include exceptions in the rule that do not require the accountant following the rule to do something that will not achieve the desired end. The consequence of such an approach is that the rules in standards may be complex because they include exceptions to the general rule where something is required to be done differently in certain circumstances than in others. In effect this leads to a proliferation of rules. It was also suggested that where the rules in accounting standards are taken as 'rules of thumb' then instead of including exceptions in the rule the standard setter may keep the general rule intact but allow those who follow the rule to override the rule where following it will not achieve the desired ends. Judgement is to be exercised by the accountant in deciding whether to follow the rule in particular circumstances or whether to override it. Where a decision of this kind is allowed then it was argued that it makes sense to include in the standard a statement of the ends or objectives of following the standard, for these are to be used in decisions about overriding the standard. These ends or objectives would be similar in nature to the objectives or desires expressed in a conceptual framework which is meant to be used by standard setters in making decisions about what standards to promulgate.

The nature of the rule setting out requirements in accounting standards thus has implications for the kind of rule included in such standards—that is, whether it is complex and includes exceptions or whether it is simpler but can be overridden. It also has implications for whether or not a statement of objectives, understood not as simply stating the content of the standard but as setting out what is wanted in following the standard, should be included in the standard. Clearly, where a standard includes rules that are 'rules of thumb' an objective of this kind would be useful, but where a standard includes rules on the 'practice' conception it would not be necessary. There may be some other purpose in including a statement of the objective of the standard, perhaps to assure those who follow the standards that they are promulgated for 'good' reasons, which may be useful in establishing the legitimacy of the standard setter, but the purpose is not to give reasons for the accountant to decide not to follow the standard. The anatomy of standards may be affected by the underlying conception of rules in standards.

The content of standards can also be affected by the standard setter's response to the problem of ambiguity in standards. In chapter 5 the problem of ambiguity and the need for interpretation of the expressions in rule-formulations was considered. One response of including implementation guidance in the standard in order to deal with the problem of ambiguity was discussed. The inclusion of implementation guidance in accounting standards will now be considered.

IMPLEMENTATION GUIDANCE

In chapter 5 it was acknowledged that rules have to be expressed by rule-formulations and that these involve language. In order to follow a rule the language used to express the rule needs to be understood. One problem with language is that it may not be understood. Where this is the case the misunderstanding can be addressed by explaining the meaning of expressions in the rule-formulation. Another problem with language is that it may be vague. There may be different ways of understanding the expressions in the rule-formulation and disagreements about what is correct. Where standard setters are aware of this vagueness then they can indicate the rule they intended to promulgate by explaining the meaning to be attributed to expressions in the rule-formulations. In order to address both these problems the meanings of expressions in the rule-formulation can be set out in *implementation guidance* included in the accounting standard. In some standards, notably IFRS 13, the content of the standard is almost exclusively to deal with the problem of vagueness. In effect, such standards express rules of a different kind. The rules are not rules about what to do in certain circumstances, but rather *rules for the meaning of expressions* that are used in other accounting standards. Such standards are really to be understood as almost exclusively implementation guidance. It was explained that implementation guidance gives an interpretation of the meaning of expressions in rule-formulations. In effect, it informs those who wish to follow the rule in the standard what the rule actually *is*. The judgement required in making a decision about the meaning of expressions in the rule-formulation is exercised by the standard setter. No judgement of this kind is expected to be exercised by those who follow the standard, for the point of implementation guidance is to eliminate the need for such judgement.

There are different kinds of vagueness that might affect accounting standards. Such vagueness may be actual—that is, there may be actual disagreements 1in understanding the rule-formulation—there may be probable vagueness, where although expressions are not differently understood in practice they may become so if applied in certain circumstances, and there may be possible vagueness, which might occur when rule-formulations are applied to new circumstances not envisaged at the time the standard was promulgated. Implementation guidance may attempt to address any of the three kinds of vagueness. The purpose of the guidance adopted by standard setters has implications for the kind of standard that emerges. Voluminous guidance sometimes arises out of a purpose of eliminating possible vagueness or, as it was also described, out of a purpose of achieving determinacy of sense. Standards of this kind may exemplify one of the characteristics of 'rules-based' standards. It was suggested, following the arguments of Wittgenstein, that this is an impossible purpose and that having such a purpose is essentially misconceived. If the motivation for 'rules-based' standards is this purpose then they are essentially misconceived. It was also argued that although determinacy of sense is an impossible ideal it does not follow that all rules in standards require the exercise of judgement in interpreting the standard. It may be that rule-formulations in standards are not actually vague, or even possibly vague, and, hence, there may be no judgements to be exercised in following them. There may be no need for implementation guidance to eliminate vagueness.

It is possible that where there is a problem of vagueness it is not addressed by standard setters through implementation guidance. Instead they may leave it to those who follow standards to interpret the standard using their judgement. It was suggested that this amounted to determining what the rule expressed by the rule-formulation *actually is*. In effect, the standard setter is leaving it to those who follow the standard to act like standard setters in promulgating a rule. However, as was also suggested, constraints are put on determining the rule by the allowable meanings of expressions in the rule-formulations. Given that those who follow rules act like standard setters in determining the rule, subject to these constraints, it makes sense to guide them in making this kind of decision about rules by informing them of the objective underlying the determination of the rule in the first place. This provides another reason for including a statement of objectives, understood as a statement of what is wanted from promulgating a rule in an accounting standard, in the standard itself. Obviously, if rule-formulations in standards are not actually or possibly vague no implementation guidance of this kind may be needed in a standard and no objectives are required in order to interpret such rule-formulations. Where there is vagueness of these kinds and where standard setters try to deal with it then more or less implementation guidance or objectives may be included in a standard. The anatomy of a standard may be affected by assumptions about the language used in standards and how certain kinds of vagueness are to be dealt with.

As an addendum, it was also argued that differences in following rules can arise not because a rule uses a vague expression but because the expressions used in standards may be explained by setting out alternatives. Implementation guidance may be used to adjudicate between these alternatives, or objectives may be given in standards where it is left to those who follow the standards to exercise judgement in deciding from amongst these alternatives which one to follow.

WHENCE OBJECTIVES?

This analysis suggests there may be different motives for the inclusion of objectives in standards, understood as elements that express what is wanted in following a rule in a standard, given the different underlying assumptions that may be made by standard setters about the kinds of rules in standards and about how to deal with vagueness of various kinds in standards. It is not clear whether the IASB includes objectives in standards to deal with the problems discussed here. Given that the objectives they include in standards are not, as argued in the previous chapter, of this kind, then the objectives in their standards would not assist in resolving problems of this kind. It is not clear why they include such objectives in their standards. The anatomy of IASB standards includes objectives but apparently only to signal the content of the standard.

SUMMARY

Accounting standards can differ in their anatomy—that is, in what is included in standards, because they have different purposes. One purpose of standards is to prescribe what is to be done in certain circumstances. These requirements are expressed in rules that are to be followed. Requirements in this sense need not be included in standards. 'Principles-only' standards may express the end to be achieved by action without specifying what the actions are. Where requirements are included in standards the rules may be different in so far as they may be conceived on the 'practice' conception or as 'rules of thumb'. Where the former is the case then exceptions, or a profusion of rules covering different circumstances, may be included in a standard. Where the latter is the case exceptions may not be included but objectives may be expressed in a standard in order to guide those who follow standards in deciding whether or not to override them. Where standards contain rule-formulations that are vague, implementation guidance may be included in standards. If it is left to the judgment of those who follow standards to interpret those standards then objectives may be included in standards to guide them in exercising judgement. Decisions about the kind of rules in standards or how to deal with problems of vagueness thus have implications for whether or not objectives are included in accounting standards.

8 Implications for Standard Setters

In regulating accounting, decisions have to be made. Accounting regulators have to decide what standards to promulgate and what is to be included in those standards. Those who follow accounting standards have to decide what to do given the standards promulgated by the standard setter. What they have to decide depends upon what is promulgated in standards. In the previous chapter the anatomy of accounting standards was considered. Standards can include rules that set out requirements. These can be conceived in different ways that can affect what the follower of such standards had to decide. Standards can also include implementation guidance that, similarly, affects what has to be decided in following standards. The inclusion of objectives in standards may be relevant to the kinds of decisions followers of standards need to make. A grasp of the issues that arise in connection with such decisions is important to both the standard setter in setting standards and to those who follow those standards. This chapter will explore these issues.

It was suggested in chapter 2 that decision-making, as it is understood in this context, is deciding to perform an intentional action, which involves coming to have a desire to act in a certain way *as a result of reasoning*. The action of accounting regulators is deciding what standards to promulgate. This will be examined first.

THE ACTIONS OF ACCOUNTING REGULATORS

It was argued in chapter 3 that decisions about which standards to promulgate are intentional actions that are done for reasons. Understanding the reasons for such actions is a matter of understanding the reasoning involved in making such decisions. Two kinds of logic are involved in such reasoning. The first is a 'logic of appropriateness' where the promulgation of specific rules of accounting is derived from more general rules. The second is a 'logic of consequences' where the reasoning is from certain ends or objectives to the desire to adopt specific rules that will meet these ends. These two kinds of logic are present in two different 'theories' of accounting that may be used in making decisions about setting standards. One kind of 'theory', and one kind of 'theorising' about accounting, involves identifying general rules to be used in deriving more specific rules that appear in accounting standards. Such theories provide 'principles' that enable decision-making that involves a 'logic of appropriateness'. Another kind of 'theory', and 'theorising', involves the identification of what is wanted from the activity of accounting and financial reporting—that is, the identification of the ends or objectives or desires to be achieved by this activity. Theories of this kind provide 'principles' that enable decision-making that involves a 'logic of consequences'. There are thus two different kinds of 'principles' that may be expressed in theories of accounting.

Standard setters need to determine what kind of theory, what kind of logic and what kind of 'principles' they are to use in making decisions about setting standards. It was suggested that the history of regulation shows that standard setters have had different conceptions of what determines such decisions. Regulation was originally seen as a matter of using a 'theory' that included 'principles'—general rules from which, using a 'logic of appropriateness', specific rules to be promulgated in standards were derived. With the move to a 'decision-usefulness' approach to standard setting— exemplified in the approach that uses a conceptual framework to assist in making decisions about standards by starting with 'principles' of accounting that express what is wanted from the activity of following standards in a 'logic of consequences'—a different kind of 'theory' emerged. It was argued that such a transition has not been fully realized and that there still may be elements of 'theorising' from general rules in conceptual frameworks. It was also argued that the failure to understand the distinction between these two approaches has resulted in ambiguities in understanding the idea of a 'principle' in conceptual frameworks. A consequence of this ambiguity is a lack of clarity amongst standard setters as to the kind of approach they are adopting in setting standards. There is little apparent awareness amongst standard setters of these two kinds of approach and the related concepts associated with them. One lesson for standard setters is that a greater appreciation of the kind of logic used in standard setting decisions and/or the nature of the 'theory' and 'theorising' implied by the use of conceptual frameworks in standard setting decisions is required. Explanations of conceptual frameworks given by standard setters who use such frameworks are deficient in not adjudicating on these issues. It is evident that there is a need to consider the nature of a conceptual framework further. Unfortunately, this is unlikely to be considered by standard setters in the near future, given the current project to revisit the conceptual framework. The IASB and the FASB decided not to investigate these issues and rejected more fundamental thinking about the nature of such frameworks when they undertook the project.

Another issue relating to the nature of the 'logic' and reasoning involved in standard setting decisions is whether or not they involve deduction. This is a question that arises where either a 'logic of appropriateness' or a 'logic of consequences' is involved. The issues that arise with both these kinds of logic were examined in chapter 3. Where decision-making involves reasoning from general to specific rules it was argued that although on one view it might be assumed that specific rules can be deduced from general rules it may be that the general rules were not to be understood as rules that must always be followed—that is, conceived as rules on the 'practice' conception—but rather might be conceived as 'rules of thumb' which might be followed in general but might be overridden by other general rules in deriving more specific rules. If general rules are conceived like this then deriving specific rules from them is not done using deductive reasoning, for the admission of other general rules as premises in the reasoning undermines the conclusion of specific rules. This is a feature of nondeductive but not deductive reasoning. A similar argument can be made for conceiving of the reasoning involved in a 'logic of consequences' as nondeductive. In order to be conceived as deductive reasoning the desires or objectives need to be considered as 'universal principles' along the lines of 'universal principles' or 'categorical imperatives' in some kinds of moral philosophy. It was argued that identifying such 'principles' that can be used in making standard setting decisions was problematic, and doubts were expressed as to whether the 'principles' in conceptual frameworks were really of this kind and were actually used in deducing desires to promulgate specific accounting standards.

These arguments suggest that another thing standard setters need to determine is the nature of the reasoning from 'principles' to standard setting decisions within either a 'logic of appropriateness' or a 'logic of consequences'. They need to understand what kind of premises they are reasoning from and what other premises might be relevant to deriving conclusions about what standards they wish to promulgate. Although there is evidence of an assumption that the reasoning involved is deductive, actual standard setting decisions are not necessarily made using such reasoning. Little attempt is made by standard setters to understand the nature of alternative kinds of reasoning and the implications it has for standard setting decisions. Although there is some consideration of these issues in the academic accounting literature this is an underdeveloped area and appears to have had little impact on standard setters.

THE ACTIONS OF THOSE WHO FOLLOW STANDARDS

In the anatomy of accounting standards an important component of standards was the expression of requirements that set out rules those who apply accounting standards must follow. In chapter 4 the different kinds of rules that may appear in standards were identified and the decisions that may need to be made relating to these different standards were reviewed. It was argued that where the rules in standards were conceived as 'rules of thumb' then a decision as to whether or not to override the requirements needs to be made by those who follow the standard. This exercise of judgement is guided by a grasp of the objectives of the standard, understood as the ends or desires to be achieved by following the requirements. As the kind of reasoning from these objectives to standards undertaken by standard setters may not be deductive, so too the reasoning from objectives to the decision to override a standard may not be deductive. A similar point may be made about interpreting the rule-formulations in standards where there is some form of vagueness. This may involve reasoning from objectives to the desire to interpret the rule-formulation, and hence the rule, in a certain way which is not deductive. Again, judgement may need to be exercised in making decisions of this kind.

A grasp of the kinds of rules in standards is important for standard setters. They need to decide whether the rules they promulgate are 'rules of thumb' or rules on the 'practice' conception. This will determine how they propose to deal with circumstances where following the rule in the standard will not achieve the objectives of the standard. It may lead to an exercise of judgement by standard setters in deciding whether or not to include exceptions in a standard. Exceptions may be included to exclude such circumstances from the ambit of the rule. Alternatively, they may decide to allow those who follow the standards to override the standard in such circumstances and not include exceptions in the rule. It was suggested that unless standard setters determine how to deal with this problem and, hence, how to determine the kind of rules they will promulgate, convergence of standards will be difficult to achieve. It is not possible to converge on a common set of standards without convergence on the kinds of rules that are promulgated in converged standards. It is surprising to find little overt discussion amongst standard setters involved in the convergence project about this issue.

Another kind of decision that may need to be made by those who follow the requirements of a standard relates to interpreting such standards. In chapter 5 it was suggested that where the expressions used in rule-formulations are vague then the meaning intended by standard setters can be made clear through implementation guidance. The purpose of including such guidance needs to be agreed upon. Standard setters need to be clear whether they are using implementation guidance to eliminate actual, possible or possible vagueness. It was argued that having the purpose of eliminating possible vagueness is misconceived and may result in the voluminous, if ineffective, guidance that characterizes 'rules-based' standards. The amount of guidance needed depends, in part, upon this purpose, and standard setters need to be aware of the different purposes and the consequences of adopting them. The alternative to the standard setter using his judgement to eliminate vagueness is to leave it to those who follow the standards to interpret the expressions in the rule-formulations themselves, guided by a grasp of the objective of the standard. Where this is done the need for implementation guidance is eliminated or reduced, thus having an impact on the content of accounting standards. Once again, the reasoning to an interpretation of a standard may not be deductive. It may be the nondeductive practical reasoning evident in a 'logic of consequences' of the kind that may have been adopted by standard setters in promulgating the standard in the first place.

The strategy adopted by standard setters in dealing with both these problems may give rise to different kinds of accounting standard being promulgated. The current literature identifies two kinds of standards that have been referred to at various points in the discussion in previous chapters, namely 'rules-based' and 'principles-based' standards.

KINDS OF STANDARD SETTING SYSTEMS

It is important to realize that the accounting standards promulgated and the kinds of standard that might emerge are dependent upon decisions about how to deal with the problems identified in the previous sections. Where rules are conceived on the 'practice' conception and exceptions are included in standards to deal with circumstances where following the rule will not achieve the desired ends, and where the strategy to deal with vagueness is to include implementation guidance where the purpose is to eliminate possible vagueness or to achieve 'determinacy of sense', then the standards may end up with many exceptions and with voluminous implementation guidance and no need for the exercise of judgement by those following the standards. Such standards may exemplify a number of the characteristics of 'rules-based' standards. This kind of standard stands in contrast to 'principles-based' standards. These are standards that have the characteristics of having few, if any, exceptions, including minimal guidance and requiring the exercise of judgement. Standards which contain 'rules of thumb' may not require the inclusion of exceptions. Those which are to be interpreted by those who follow them may not need to include much in the way of implementation guidance. Both require the exercise of judgement to deal with the problems of rules that do not always achieve the desired ends and vagueness. The kind of system to be adopted by standard setters is dependent on the answers they give to dealing with such problems.

Although there is much talk about the need to exercise judgement in following standards there is little overt discussion of the kind of judgement and decisions that need to be made in exercising such judgement. Indeed, although 'principles-based' standards are characterized as those which require the exercise of judgement there is little overt discussion about the kind of judgement involved. This raises doubts about whether the almost universal agreement about the desirability of 'principles-based' standards is actually agreement about the desirability of the same kind of thing. A conceptual enquiry into the meaning of 'judgement' in this context is clearly required to be undertaken by standard setters who support the promulgation of standards that are to be 'principles-based' and, hence, require the exercise of judgement.

Given a commitment to regulation of activities, the debate about different approaches to regulation and to the kind of constraints that are to be imposed by bodies other than those who are subject to the regulations or those that are affected by the actions that are to be regulated has been with us in different contexts for many years. In the accounting literature these approaches have been characterized as a 'rules-based' versus a 'principles-based' approach. It has also been referred to as a contrast between a 'formalist' and an 'anti-formalist' approach. The latter implies 'a narrow approach to legal control—the use of clearly defined, highly administrable rules, an emphasis on uniformity, consistency and predictability, on the legal form of transactions and relationships and on literal interpretation' (McBarnet and Whelan, 1991, p. 80). An 'anti-formalist' approach puts 'the emphasis on capturing and controlling the substance rather than the form of a real life transaction or relationship, and implementing the spirit rather than the letter of the law'. This involves stressing 'the purpose of the law', the use of 'broad criteria', the 'avoidance of tight definitions' and reliance on the profession for 'fleshing out the details of accounting regulation' (McBarnet and Whelan, 1991, pp. 86–87). The similarity of the criteria used to explain an 'anti-formalist' standard with those used to explain a 'principles-based' standard is evident particularly if the 'fleshing out of details' involves the use of judgement and where the 'purpose of the law' is equivalent to the objectives of the law or, in the accounting context, the rule in the standard.

The debate about the approach to regulation is not confined to the regulation of accounting and financial reporting. In other contexts there are similar arguments about regulating activities, and similar issues arise. Two examples will be briefly reviewed.

EXAMPLES OF APPROACHES TO REGULATION IN OTHER CONTEXTS

In Wagner's opera *Die Meistersinger von Nurnberg* there is a debate about the correct way to regulate the activity of singing. The Mastersingers guild regulates singing through a collection of detailed prescriptions about what kind of song is acceptable in a song competition. A debate ensues about this approach to regulation when an outsider, Walther von Stolzing, attempts to enter the competition for the best song and so gain entry into the guild of Mastersingers. The problem is that his song does not follow the rules of singing and a number of Mastersingers do not think him worthy of being admitted to the guild. One member, Hans Sachs, a shoemaker with philosophical interests, recognises that the song is actually genuine art even though it flouts the rules. In effect, it follows 'Nature's law', which Sachs recognises was the original objective the rules developed by the guild were meant to achieve. Walther rejects these rules when he says, 'Oh Heaven, teach me no cobbler's trade—rather tell me how a singer's made' (English

National Opera (ENO) and The Royal Opera (TRO), 1983). This debate raises several questions. Who should determine what the rules of singing should be, and what objectives should be agreed as to what the rules should achieve? If a song does not follow the rules then can the rule be overridden as long as it achieves the objectives that prompted the acceptance of the rule in the first place? These objectives—or, as they might be described, 'principles'—are indicated by the admittedly rather vague expression 'Nature'. The Mastersingers assume they are responsible for establishing the rules of singing that are to be followed. Sachs challenges this view when he suggests the Mastersingers should at least consider whether they should 'forget the laws you treasure, seek out first what his rules may be' (ENO and RHO, 1983). He thus accepts that what is important is whether or not the song achieves certain objectives and that it may be that an individual, rather than an institution like the guild of Mastersingers, should determine her own rules. He also considers that if the guild is to be given the responsibility for setting the rules then the rules should also be examined against such 'principles' regularly to determine whether they are still in accord with it or whether they need to be revised or abandoned in the light of these 'principles'. In the opera Walther's song ends up winning the prize, and he is invited to become a Master.

The initial attitude of the Mastersingers if applied to the regulation of accounting suggests an approach that might be adopted by a Mastersingers Accounting Standards Board (MASB). The idea is that accounting and financial reporting are regulated by an institution, a standard setter, who develops rules by consideration of some underlying objectives. The rules, once developed, have to be strictly followed. No override is allowed. No interpretation by those who follow them is encouraged, for the guild is the arbiter or judge of what is acceptable in following the rules. In effect, this is a 'rules-based' approach. It is contrasted with the approach of Walther, who grasps the objectives of the rules and develops his own rules which meet the objectives. This is, in effect, self-regulation—that is, no real regulation—as defined by Taylor and Turley and quoted at the start of the book. There are different 'half-way' houses. One approach would be to regulate the activity by setting out the objectives that are to be achieved by the actions to be undertaken and prescribing only that those who are subject to regulation 'do something that will achieve the objectives'. It is then up to those who follow the prescription to decide what to do either on a case-by-case basis or by establishing their own rules to guide their actions. This might be dubbed a 'principles-only' approach. Another approach is for standard setters to set out the rules but regularly review them against the objectives to determine whether or not the rules should be changed in so far as they do or do not achieve the objectives underlying them. This might be thought to be the approach of the IASB in which the standard setter is meant to review whether following the standards achieves the desired outcome in a 'post-implementation review'. Alternatively, the rules of standard setters can stand but an override or an interpretation of the rule-formulation be allowed where, in particular circumstances, following the rule or adopting an alternative interpretation would not achieve the objectives of the standard. Both these approaches might be dubbed 'principles-based'.

Another context where the debate about regulation has occurred is in the New Testament where the Pharisees and Jesus argue about what actions are and are not allowable. The Pharisees insist on the observance of a rule not to heal or perform certain acts on the Sabbath. Jesus argues that the rule should not apply where following the rule will frustrate the ends for which the laws were established. The rules against doing certain things on the Sabbath were established with the intention of 'doing good' where this is understood as achieving the two most important commandments, 'Love the Lord your God with all your heart and with all your soul and with all your mind and with all your strength' and 'Love your neighbour as yourself'. These two 'commandments' might be understood as two 'principles' that set out what is to be achieved by actions undertaken. The prescription is to 'do something that will . . . ' where . . . ' is filled in with the objective of 'loving God' or 'loving your neighbour'.

Once again there are different ways of characterizing these approaches. The Pharisees' approach is one that, like the approach of the Mastersingers, recognises the Pharisees as the institution responsible for establishing, or at least implementing, the rules. Apparently, there were 613 individual statutes in the law applied by the Pharisees (*NIV Study Bible*, 1985, p. 1489). It might be argued that the objectives of these rules had become irrelevant. No override of the rules is allowed by considering, on particular occasions, whether or not following the rule will achieve the objectives. No interpretation by those following the rules is allowed, for the Pharisees were the arbiter of the meaning of the rule-formulations. The absence of consideration of the objectives of the rules is the point Jesus is making about the rules in terms of what is to be done on the Sabbath. Jesus's approach could be called a 'principles-only' approach given that although the objective to be achieved by 'doing something . . . ' is set out, there is no guidance about what has to be done. Arguably the 'guidance' about what is to be done is given by examples and parables that *show* what will achieve the objectives rather than through rules of conduct that *say* what has to be done. The contrast between these two systems has been called 'an important binary in the New Testament' and is characterized as 'the opposition between law and love. Accordingly, the New Testament, particularly the Synoptic Gospels, presents especially the leadership of the Pharisees as obsessed with man-made rules (especially concerning purity) whereas Jesus is more concerned with God's love'. The word 'pharisee' has come to mean 'a hypocritical and arrogant person who places the letter of the law above its spirit' (Wikipedia, 2013). Applied to the approach to the regulation of accounting and financial reporting this might resolve into a contrast between a Pharisees Accounting Standards Board (PhASB) and a 'principles-only' system.

Both these examples suggest that standard setters in the area of accounting and financial reporting need to explore the issues considered throughout this book that arise in connection with such decisions. These issues are important to both the standard setter in setting standards and to those who follow those standards. More fundamental thinking about the approach to regulation is required. Considering other contexts may sharpen appreciation of what is involved.

SUMMARY AND CONCLUDING REMARKS

An understanding of the nature of decision-making in standard setting is necessary for standard setters. They need to determine what kind of theory, what kind of logic and what kind of 'principles' are to be used in making decisions about setting standards. In particular, they need to determine whether they will base their decisions on theories that set out general rules of accounting or on theories that set out what is to be achieved—the ends, objectives or desires that are to be fulfilled—through promulgating accounting standards. It is also important for standard setters to determine what kind of rules or prescriptions they will include in accounting standards where they decide to promulgate prescriptions about what to do in standards. They need to decide whether the rules they include are rules on the 'practice' conception or 'rules of thumb' and whether or not to allow those who follow standards to override the requirements in standards. They also need to decide how to deal with problems of vagueness—that is, whether to leave it to those who follow the standards to interpret the rule-formulations or to include implementation guidance that attempts to deal with vagueness. They need to decide what kind of vagueness they wish to deal with when including implementation guidance in standards. Decisions of this kind involve a more general decision about how much judgement to allow to those who follow standards and how much judgement is to be exercised by standard setters in dealing with these problems. Different approaches to these issues and their resolution are identified with help from examples from opera and the New Testament. These throw light on the nature of accounting regulation and the different approaches that might be taken to it.

This book has undertaken conceptual enquiry into a number of concepts that are used in thinking about the nature of accounting regulation. It has been suggested at various points that the confusions or uncertainties in accounting regulation arise from a failure of standard setters and academics to undertake adequate conceptual enquiry. One objective of the book is to facilitate greater understanding of the concepts of intentional actions and decision-making, conceptual frameworks, accounting theories and 'principles' of accounting, rules and different conceptions of rules, different kinds of reasoning involved in standard setting and in following standards, interpretation and implementation guidance and judgement and its exercise.

One common theme that has emerged in the course of the book is that decisions that have to be made by standard setters and by those who follow standards involve reasoning that is not deductive. Indeed, it was suggested that decision-making is actually a process of reasoning to a desire to perform some action, whether of promulgating a standard, overriding a requirement or interpreting a rule-formulation. It was also suggested that the idea of exercising judgement is precisely the process of reasoning in a nondeductive manner. Drawing conclusions in such reasoning is not concluding something that is necessary in the way it is with deductive reasoning. Some decisions or choices have to be made in drawing conclusions, which characterises such reasoning as involving judgement.

The book began by considering the nature of accounting and examined what it meant to say that accounting is an intentional action. Insights from the philosophical literature were used in a conceptual enquiry into intentional actions, which were identified as those actions that are done for reasons. Having a reason involves wanting to do something to bring about a certain result and believing the action contemplated will bring about this result. It was then suggested that the actions of accountants and preparers of financial statements are performed, these days, because there is a practice of following a rule that has been adopted to determine what is to be done in certain accounting circumstances. The rule forms part of the reason for undertaking the actions of accounting and financial reporting. Different kinds of practices were identified, and accounting has been said to be an institutional or legal practice where the pronouncements of standard setting institutions like the IASB or FASB set out the rules that are followed in practice. Where such practices exist it is possible to ask further questions about why individual accountants or preparers perform accounting and financial reporting actions. Such questioning may be designed to elicit reasons accountants want to follow the rules promulgated by standard setters, but another reason for asking the question is to elicit reasons standard setters promulgate the rules that are followed.

Asking the latter kind of question constitutes an attempt to elicit the 'theoretical' backing for standard setting decisions. The nature of 'theories' of this kind was examined in a conceptual enquiry into 'accounting theories' and 'theorization'. It was suggested that the theories that underpin such decisions are not to be understood as scientific theories used in explanation and prediction of events but rather as eliciting reasons for the standard setter's actions of promulgating accounting standards. Given that such standards include rules, this kind of theorizing should be understood as normative theorizing, in the sense that it is some kind of thinking about norms or rules to be adopted. This should be understood as reasoning to the desire to adopt rules. It was suggested that the adoption of a rule amounts to a desire to act in a certain way in general whenever certain circumstances exist. The reasons that underpin the desire to adopt a rule must include both desires and beliefs, as was required in reasoning to particular intentional actions, but they must also have a certain generality. The desires underpinning the adoption of a rule must include a desire to do something in general and beliefs that following the rule will, in general, fulfil these desires. This provided a way of understanding the nature of a conceptual framework. One conception of a conceptual framework is that it is the kind of theory that expresses general desires underpinning standard setting decisions. An alternative conception of it is that it is something that sets out general rules from which the more specific rules expressed in accounting standards are derived. The nature of the reasoning used in standard setting decisions was examined. It was suggested that where such decisions are made by considering desires to be achieved by the standards in question, the reasoning, like the reasoning underpinning particular intentional actions, should not be conceived of as deductive reasoning but as a form of practical reasoning. Insights from moral philosophy were used to throw light on this kind of reasoning and on the premises a conceptual framework expresses that are used in such reasoning. It was suggested that conceptual frameworks might express both general desires as well as general rules used by standard setters in deriving desires to promulgate accounting standards. It was suggested that 'principles' of the kind included in conceptual frameworks can be understood as expressions of desires or expressions of general rules that are used in standard setting decisions. Decision-making in the context of standard setting is reasoning to the desire to promulgate accounting standards. The analysis of reasons and reasoning in decision-making of this kind throws light on the nature of conceptual frameworks and their purpose. It was suggested that where 'principles' are expressions of desires which are used in practical reasoning to the desire to promulgate rules, decisions may need to be made in deriving such rules given that the reasoning concerned is not deductive. Conceptual enquiry into the concepts of 'reasons', 'reasoning' and 'principles' throws light on the concept of a 'conceptual framework' itself.

Having clarified the nature of the conceptual framework, the book considered how the 'principles' in such a framework are used to make standard setting decisions. Given the desires expressed in the framework or the general rules, specific rules are derived by considering beliefs as to what rules will, in general, fulfil the desires expressed in practical reasoning or the meaning of expressions in general rules which allow the derivation of more specific rules. It was suggested that where particular rules will not fulfil the desires that constitute premises in practical reasoning on all occasions, standard setters may still decide to promulgate a rule. Either they do not worry about those occasions on which the rule will not achieve the desired end or they are concerned and either include exceptions within the rule to exclude those instances from the ambit of the rule or allow the rule to be treated as a 'rule of thumb'. The book distinguished 'rules of thumb' from rules on the 'practice' conception as part of a conceptual enquiry into 'rule'. When a rule is conceived as a 'rule of thumb' an override of the rule is allowed in those instances where following the rule would not achieve the desired end. It was also suggested that general rules used in reasoning to particular rules might also be conceived not as rules on the 'practice' conception but as 'rules of thumb'. This means it may be necessary to weigh general rules and decide which of the general rules are to be used to derive more specific rules. This means standard setters may need to make decisions about the particular rules to be derived from general rules given that the reasoning is not deductive. Where particular rules are derived from more general 'rules of thumb' or where 'rules of thumb' are derived from desires in conjunction with beliefs that following a rule will not meet the desire on all occasions then individual accountants or preparers of financial statements may have to exercise judgement in making decisions about whether or not to follow the rule or override it on particular occasions. The reasoning from rules to a desire to act in accord with a rule in a 'logic of appropriateness' is not, in such cases, deductive.

Further problems that exist for standard setters relate to the nature of the language used to formulate rules in accounting standards. Where the language is vague or indeterminate in meaning the rule-formulation may be interpreted in different ways by those who follow the rule. It was suggested, following the insights provided by philosophy, that this means the rule expressed by the rule-formulation may be taken as different by different followers of the rule. This may result in a lack of comparability in actions in accord with the rule, which affects the comparability of financial statements drawn up in accordance with the rule. There are two general ways in which standard setters can overcome this problem. They can allow those who follow the rule to interpret the rule-formulation guided by a grasp of the objective or desires to be achieved by following the rule. This allows judgement to be exercised by those who follow the rules to determine what the rule is given the rule-formulation and a grasp of the objectives of the rule. The kind of judgement arises because the followers of the rule are, in effect, making a similar kind of standard setting decision to standard setters promulgating a standard. The reasoning involved is nondeductive practical reasoning from desires and beliefs to a desire to act. Alternatively, they can include implementation guidance in the accounting standard to explain how the expressions in the rule-formulation are to be understood. In order to understand this a conceptual enquiry into 'implementation guidance' and 'meaning' was undertaken. Problems with such implementation guidance are explored including the difficulty that the explanations of the meaning of expression in the rule-formulation can themselves be misunderstood. The attempt to forestall such problems by including even more implementation guidance runs up against the problems of indeterminacy. It was argued that the attempt to achieve determinacy of sense lies behind one of the motivations towards 'rules-based' accounting standards. It is essentially misconceived.

The analysis of different kinds of rules that may be expressed in standards and of the possible vagueness in the language used to express the rules throws light on the anatomy of accounting standards and of the different kinds of standards that may be promulgated. It also throws light on the idea of 'principles-based' standards and the distinction between these kind of standards and 'rules-based' standards. The idea that 'principles-based' standards are those that involve the exercise of judgement is explained by highlighting the need to exercise judgement in following rules that are 'rules of thumb' and in following rules that use expressions that are vague. The explanation of how conceptual frameworks are used in making standard setting decisions also throws light upon the idea of 'principles-based' standards as those that are based on conceptual frameworks. The analysis of reasons and reasoning in explaining the use of such frameworks in making standard setting decisions clarifies the suggestion that using such frameworks to make these kinds of decisions involves the exercise of judgement, albeit by the standard setter. It was suggested that the idea of a 'principles-based' standard can be understood in various ways and that different kinds of judgement exercised by different groups of people may be involved. The failure to undertake conceptual enquiry into the concept of 'principles-based' and 'rules-based' standards has undermined understanding of the different kinds of standards and of the reasons for adopting them. Understanding such standards is not assisted by the claim that 'principles-based' standards are those that involve the exercise of judgement, for such judgement can be of a different kind and exercised by different people. A suggestion for clarifying the idea of judgement is that judgement is exercised in decision-making because the reasoning to decisions that is involved in decision-making is not deductive. Certain decisions or choices need to be made in reasoning that is not deductive which do not need to be made where reasoning is deductive. Because the nature of decision-making has not been adequately explained the different kinds of decision-making and the different kinds of reasoning to decisions have not been clearly grasped. Again, a conceptual enquiry into 'judgement' clarifies the nature of decision-making.

The failure to conduct adequate conceptual enquiry has been responsible for the failure to adequately explain and grasp the nature of accounting regulation. The interests of standard setters in promulgating appropriate standards from an appropriate framework have not always been usefully directed because of the confusions concerning important concepts used in structuring thinking about standards. In the rush to produce conceptual frameworks and accounting standards to regulate accounting, standard setters have ignored the 'hygiene' of conceptual enquiry. They have made claims for conceptual frameworks that cannot be achieved in practice. This has undermined faith in their operation. Different standard setters are unable to achieve convergence on standards because they have not achieved convergence on the underlying theory underpinning standard setting decisions and have not been able to agree on the kind of standards thought to be ideal. This is partly due to the rather slovenly attitude they have taken towards the language with which debates about frameworks and standards have been conducted. In consequence they have been unable to 'unravel the knots' in their thinking about these things. This book has attempted to use conceptual enquiry to bring such language back from a 'holiday' it has been on for some years and to employ the concepts newly understood, once again, in useful work. It has tried to show that some of the issues that arise in standard setting can be better addressed if the concepts employed in discussions are better understood. In the Preface to *Philosophical Investigations*, where such an enquiry is undertaken into concepts that have been important in philosophy, Wittgenstein wrote, 'It is not impossible that it should fall to the lot of this work, in its poverty and in the darkness of this time, to bring light into one brain or another—but, of course, it is not likely' (Wittgenstein, 1953, Preface). This work is presented with a little more optimism. . . .

References

AAA (1977) *Statement on accounting theory and theory acceptance.* Evanston, IL: AAA.

AAA (2003) 'Evaluating concepts-based vs. rules-based approaches to standard setting', *Accounting Horizons*, 17(1), pp. 73–89.

ACIFR (2008) *Final report of the advisory committee on improvements to financial reporting to the United States Securities and Exchange Commission.* Washington, DC: SEC. Available at: http://www.sec.gov/about/offices/oca/acifr/acifr-finalreport.pdf [Accessed 25 January 2013].

Alexander, D. (1999) 'A benchmark for the adequacy of published financial statements', *Accounting and Business Research*, 29(3), pp. 239–253.

Alexander, D., Britton, A. and Jorissen, A. (2011) *International financial reporting and analysis.* 5th ed. Andover, England: South-Western CENGAGE Learning.

Alexander, D. and Jermakowicz, E. (2006) 'A true and fair view of the principles/rules debate', *ABACUS*, 42(2), pp. 132–164.

Anscombe, G.E.M. (1957) *Intention.* Oxford: Basil Blackwell.

APB (1970) 'Basic concepts and accounting principles underlying financial statements of business enterprises', *Accounting Principles Board Statement No.4.* New York: AICPA.

Archer, S. (1993) 'On the methodology of constructing a conceptual framework for financial accounting', in Mumford, M. and Peasnell, K. (ed.) (1993) *Philosophical perspectives on accounting.* London: Routledge.

Archer, S. (1998) 'Mattessich's Critique of Accounting: a review article', *Accounting and Business Research*, 28(3), pp. 297–316.

ASB (1999) *Statement of principles for financial reporting.* London: ASB.

Baker, G. and Hacker, P. (1980) *Wittgenstein: meaning and understanding.* Oxford: Blackwell.

Baker, G. and Hacker, P. (1985) *Wittgenstein: rules, grammar and necessity.* Oxford: Blackwell.

Barth, M. (2007) 'Standard-setting measurement issues and the relevance of research', *Accounting and Business Research*, Special Issue, International Accounting Policy Forum, pp. 7–15.

Baxter, W.T. (1953) 'Recommendations on accounting theory', *Accountant*, 10, October.

Baxter, W. T. (1981) 'Accounting standards—boon or curse?' *Accounting and Business Research*, Winter.

Bennett, B., Bradbury, M. and Prangnell, H. (2006) 'Rules, principles and judgments in accounting standards', *ABACUS*, 42(2), pp. 189–203.

Benston, G. J., Bromwich, M. and Wagenhofer, A. (2006) 'Principles- versus rules-based accounting standards: the FASB's standard setting strategy', *ABACUS*, 42(2), pp. 165–188.

Berry, A. (1993) *Financial accounting: an introduction.* London: Chapman & Hall.

Brown, G.A., Collins R. and Thornton, D.B. (1993) 'Professional judgment and accounting standards', *Accounting, Organizations and Society,* 18(4), pp. 275–289.

Blackburn, S. (1984) *Spreading the word.* Oxford: Clarendon Press.

Bushman, R. and Landsman, W.R. (2010) 'The pros and cons of regulating corporate reporting: a critical review of the arguments', *Accounting and Business Research,* 40(3), pp. 259–273.

Chambers, R.J. (1955) 'Blueprint for a theory of accounting', *Accounting Research, January, pp. 17-25.*

Chambers, R.J. (1966) 'The development of accounting theory', in Chambers, R.J., Goldberg, L. and Mathews, R.L. (ed.) *The accounting frontier.* London: F.W. Cheshire.

Chambers Twentieth Century Dictionary (1971). Edinburgh: W. R. Chambers Ltd.

CICA (1988) *Professional judgment in financial reporting.* Toronto: CICA.

CICA (1995) *Professional judgment and the auditor.* Toronto: CICA.

Craig, E., ed. (2005) *The shorter Routledge encyclopedia of philosophy.* Abingdon: Routledge.

Cunningham, R.A. (2007) 'A prescription to retire the rhetoric of "principles-based systems" in corporate law, securities regulation and accounting', *Vanderbilt Law Review,* 60(5), pp. 1411–1493.

Davidson, D. (1980) 'Actions, reasons and causes', in *Essays on Actions and Events.* Oxford: Oxford University Press.

Davies, M., Paterson, R. and Wilson, A. (1999) *UK GAAP.* 6th ed. Croydon: Ernst & Young.

Dean, G. and Clarke, F. (2004) 'Principles vs rules: true and fair view and IFRSs', *ABACUS,* 40(2), pp. i–iv.

Dean, G. and Clarke, F. (2005) ' "True and fair" and "fair value"—Accounting and legal will-o'-the-wisps', *ABACUS,* 41(2), pp. i–viii.

Deloitte (2006) *Highlights of the AICPA National Conference on Current SEC and PCAOB Developments, December 21, 2006.* Available at: http://www.deloitte.com/view/en_US/us/Services/audit-enterprise-risk-services/Financial-Statement-Internal-Control-Audit/Accounting-Standards-Communications/7ef7d159d9f45210VgnVCM200000bb42f00aRCRD.htm [Accessed 13 September, 2011].

Dennis, I. (2008) 'A conceptual enquiry into the concept of a "principles-based" accounting standard', *British Accounting Review,* 40(3), pp. 260–271.

Dennis, I. (2010a) ' "Clarity" begins at home: an examination of the conceptual underpinnings of the IAASB's clarity project', *International Journal of Auditing,* 14(3), pp. 294–319.

Dennis, I. (2010b) 'What do you expect? A reconfiguration of the audit expectations gap', *International Journal of Auditing,* 14(2), pp. 130–146.

DiMaggio, P.J. and Powell, W.W. (1991) 'The iron cage revisited: institutional isomorphism and collective rationality in organization fields', in Powell, W.W. and DiMaggio, P.J. (ed.) (1991) *The new institutionalism in organizational analysis.* Chicago: University of Chicago Press.

Dopuch, N. and Sunder, S. (1980) 'FASB's statements on objectives and elements of financial accounting: a review', *Accounting Review,* 55(1), pp. 1–21.

ENO and TRO (1983) *The Mastersingers of Nuremberg opera guide.* London: John Calder.

Evans, L. (2003) 'The true and fair view and the "fair presentation" override of IAS 1', *Accounting and Business Research,* 33(4), pp. 311–325.

FASB (1974) *Discussion memorandum the conceptual framework for financial accounting and reporting: elements of financial statements and their measurement.* Norwalk, Connecticut: FASB.

FASB (2001) 'Why does the FASB have a conceptual framework?' *Understanding the Issues,* August 2001. Norwalk, Connecticut: FASB.

FASB (2002) *Proposal: principles-based approach to U.S. standard setting.* Norwalk, Connecticut: FASB.

FASB (2004) *FASB response to SEC study on the adoption of a principles-based accounting system.* Norwalk, Connecticut: FASB. Accessible at: http://www.fasb.org/response_sec_study_july2004.pdf [Accessed 17 January 2012].

FASB/IASB (2005) *Revisiting the concepts: a new conceptual framework project.* Norwalk, Connecticut: FASB. Accessible at: http://www.ifrs.org/NR/rdonlyres/E5B8A298–6179–4FAA-985A-42416EB597F5/0/8_1455_0602sob04a.pdf [Accessed 12 January 2012].

FASB/IASB (2006) *Preliminary views conceptual framework for financial reporting: objective of financial reporting and qualitative characteristics of decision-useful financial reporting information.* Norwalk, Connecticut: FASB.

FASB (2010) *Statement of Financial Accounting Concepts No. 8. Conceptual Framework for Financial Reporting Chapter 1. The objective of general purpose financial reporting, and Chapter 3 Qualitative characteristics of useful financial information.* Norwalk, Connecticut: FASB.1

FEE (2007) *Selected issues in relation to financial statement audits.* Brussels: Fédération des Experts Comptables Européens. Available at: http://www.fee.be/publications/default.asp?library_ref=4&content_ref=771 [Accessed 27 May 2010].

Gleick, J. (2003) *Isaac Newton.* London: Harper Perennial.

Global Public Policy Symposium (2008) *Principles-based accounting standards.* New York: Global Public Policy Symposium. Available at: http://www.globalpublicpolicysymposium.com/documents.htm [Accessed 13 September 2011].

Goldman, A. I. (1970) *A theory of human action.* Princeton, NJ: Princeton University Press.

Hacker, P. M. S. (1996) *Wittgenstein: mind and will.* Part I, *Essays.* Oxford: Blackwell.

Hare, R. M. (1952) *The language of morals.* Oxford: Oxford University Press.

Hendriksen, E. S. (1977) *Accounting theory.* Homewood, IL: Richard D. Irwin.

Hines, R. D. (1989) 'Financial accounting knowledge, conceptual framework projects and the social construct of the accounting profession', *Accounting, Auditing and Accountability Journal,* 2(2), pp. 72–92.

Hoogervoorst, H. (2012) 'The concept of prudence: dead or alive?' Speech given at FEE Conference on Corporate Reporting of the Future, Brussels, Belgium, 18 September 2012. Accessible at: http://www.ifrs.org/Alerts/PressRelease/Documents/2012/Concept%20of%20Prudence%20speech.pdf [Accessed 25 January 2013].

IAASB (2010) *International auditing standards.* New York: IAASB.

IASB (1989) *Framework for the preparation and presentation of financial statements.* London: IASB.

IASB (2010) *The conceptual framework for financial reporting.* London: IASB.

IASB (2013) *International financial reporting standards.* London: IASB.

ICAS (2006) *Principles not rules: a question of judgment.* Edinburgh: ICAS.

Kam, V. (1990) *Accounting theory.* New York: John Wiley & Sons.

Kant, I. (1785) *Groundwork of the metaphysic of morals,* reprinted in and translated by Paton, H. J. (1948) *The moral law.* London: Hutchinson University Library.

Lemmon, E. J. (1965) *Beginning logic.* London: Nelson University Paperbacks.

Lennard, A. (2007) 'Stewardship and the objectives of financial statements: a comment on IASB's preliminary views on an improved conceptual framework for financial reporting: the objective of financial reporting and qualitative characteristics of decision-useful financial reporting information', *Accounting in Europe,* 4(1), pp. 51–66

Lyas, C. (1993) 'Accounting and language', in Mumford, M. and Peasnell, K. (ed.) (1993) *Philosophical perspectives on accounting*. London: Routledge.

Macve, R. (1983) 'The FASB's conceptual framework—Vision, tool or threat?' presented at the Arthur Young Professors' Roundtable, 7 May 1983.

March, J. G. (1994) *A primer on decision making: how decisions happen*. New York: Free Press.

Mason, A. K. and Gibbins, M. (1991) 'Judgment and U.S. accounting standards', *Accounting Horizons*, 5(2), pp. 14–24.

Mattessich, R. (1995) 'Conditional-normative accounting methodology: incorporating value judgements and means-end relations of an applied science', *Accounting, Organizations and Society*, 20(4), pp. 259–284.

McBarnet, D. and Whelan, D. (1991) 'The elusive spirit of the law: formalism and the struggle for legal control', *Modern Law Review*, November, pp. 848–873.

Miller, P. B. W. (1990) 'The conceptual framework as reformation and counter-reformation', *Accounting Horizons*, 4(2), pp. 23–32.

Moonitz, M. (1961) 'The basic postulates of accounting', *Accounting Research Study No. 1*. New York: AICPA.

Moonitz, M. and Sprouse, R. T. (1962) 'A tentative set of broad accounting principles for business enterprises', *Accounting Research Study No. 3*. New York: AICPA.

Moore, M. (2008) *The true and fair requirement revisited. Opinion*. London: FRC. Available at: http://www.frc.org.uk/documents/pagemanager/frc/T&F%20Opinion%2021%20April%202008.pdf [Accessed 20 September 2011].

Moran, M. (2010) 'The political economy of regulation: does it have any lessons for accounting research?' *Accounting and Business Research*, 40(3), pp. 215–225.

NIV Study Bible (1985). London: Hodder and Stoughton.

Nobes, C. (2005) 'Rules-based standards and the lack of principles in accounting', *Accounting Horizons*, 19(1), pp. 25–34.

Nobes, C. and Parker, R. (2006) *Comparative international accounting*. 9th ed. Harlow, England: FT Prentice Hall.

Page, M. and Spira, L. (2005) 'Ethical codes, independence and the conservation of ambiguity', *Business Ethics: A European Review*, 14(3), pp. 301–316.

Paton, H. J. (1948) *The moral law*. London: Hutchinson University Library.

Paton, W. A. (1922) *Accounting theory*. New York: Ronald Press Company.

Popper, K. (1963) Conjectures and Refutations. New York: Harper and Row.

Power, M. (1993) 'On the idea of a conceptual framework for financial reporting', in Mumford, M. and Peasnell, K. (ed.) (1993) *Philosophical perspectives on accounting*. London: Routledge.

Rawls, J. (1955) 'Two concepts of rules', *Philosophical Review*, 64, reprinted in Foot, P. (ed.) (1967) *Theories of ethics* in the *Oxford Readings in Philosophy* series. Oxford: Oxford University Press.

Salmon, W. (1992) 'Scientific explanation', in *Introduction to the philosophy of science*. Indianapolis: Hackett Publishing Company.

Schipper, K. (2003) 'Principles-based accounting standards', *Accounting Horizons*, 17(1), pp. 61–72.

Schipper, K. (2005) 'The Introduction of International Accounting Standards in Europe: Implications for International Convergence', *European Accounting Review*, 14 (1), pp. 101–126.

SEC (2003) *Study report pursuant to Section 108(d) of the Sarbanes-Oxley Act of 2002*. Accessible at: http://www.sec.gov/news/studies/principlesbasedstand.htm [Accessed 14 November 2011].

Skinner, R. (1995/2005) 'Judgment in jeopardy', first published in *CA Magazine*, November 1995, and reprinted in *Canadian Accounting Perspectives*, 4(2), 2005, pp. 143–152.

Solomons, D. (1978) 'The politicization of accounting', *Journal of Accountancy*, 146(5), pp. 65–72.

Taylor, P. and Turley, S. (1986) *The regulation of accounting*. Oxford: Basil Blackwell.

Tweedie, D. (1993) 'Preface: the accountant: a tradesman or a professional', in Mumford, M. and Peasnell, K. (ed.) (1993) *Philosophical perspectives on accounting*. London: Routledge.

Twining, W. and Miers, D. (1976) *How to do things with rules*. London: Weidenfeld and Nicolson.

Van Hulle, K. (1997) 'The true and fair view override in the European Accounting Directives', *European Accounting Review*, 6(4), pp. 711–720.

Watts, R. L. and Zimmerman, J. L. (1978) 'Towards a positive theory of the determination of accounting standards', *Accounting Review*, 53(1), pp. 112–134.

West, B. (2003) *Professionalism and accounting rules*. London: Routledge.

Wikipedia (2011). *Algorithm*. Accessible at: http://en.wikipedia.org/wiki/Algorithm [Accessed 25 January 2013].

Wikipedia (2013) *Pharisees*. Accessible at: http://en.wikipedia.org/wiki/Pharisees [Accessed 25 January 2013].

Wittgenstein, L. (1953) *Philosophical investigations*. Oxford: Basil Blackwell.

Wittgenstein, L. (1969) *On certainty*. Oxford: Basil Blackwell.

Wüstemann, J. and Wüstemann, S. (2010) 'Why consistency of accounting standards matters: a contribution to the rules-versus-principles debate in financial reporting', *ABACUS*, 46(1), pp. 1–27.

Young, J. (2006) 'Making up users', *Accounting, Organizations and Society*, 31(6), pp. 579–600.

Zeff, S. A. (1972) *Forging accounting principles in five countries: a history and an analysis of trends. Accounting Lectures 1971*. Champaign, IL: Stipes Publishing.

Zeff, S. A. (1978) 'The rise of "economic consequences" ', *Journal of Accountancy*, 146(6), pp. 56–63.

Zeff, S. A. (1990) 'The English-language equivalent of Geeft een Getrouw Beeld', in Parker, R. H. and Nobes, C. W. (1994) *An international view of true and fair accounting*. London: Routledge.

Zeff, S. A. (1999) 'The evolution of the conceptual framework for business enterprises in the United States', *Accounting Historians Journal*, 26(2), pp. 89–131.

Zeff, S. A. (2002) ' "Political" lobbying on proposed standards: a challenge to the IASB', *Accounting Horizons*, 16(1), pp. 43–54.

Index